PRESENTING YOURSELF

A Personal Image Guide for MEN

PRESENTING YOURSELF

A Personal Image Guide for MEN

Mary Spillane

from CMB Image Consultants

PIATKUS

© 1993 Mary Spillane
CMB is a registered trademark of
Color Me Beautiful Inc.

First published in 1993 by
Judy Piatkus (Publishers) Ltd
5 Windmill Street, London W1P 1HF

**The moral right of the author
has been asserted**

*A catalogue record for this book is
available from the British Library*

ISBN 0−7499−1309−6
ISBN 0−7499−1282−0(Pbk)

Designed by Paul Saunders
Line drawings by Paul Saunders
Illustrations of suits, suit details and
    shirt collars by Pascale Laurent
Photography by Iain Philpott and
    (pages 41, 43, 45, 47, 49, 51 and 95)
    Graeme Montgomery
Hair and Make-up by Martin Fletcher
(See also Picture Credits on page 168)

Set in Linotron Century Old Style
Typesetting, reproduction and
electronic manipulation by
Create Publishing Services, Bath
Printed and bound in Great Britain by
Bath Press Colourbooks, Blantyre, Scotland

This book is dedicated to my husband, Roger, who provided valued perspectives as an international businessman. Despite years of ongoing 'suggestions' about his image and unsolicited alterations to his wardrobe, he remains my best friend.

CONTENTS

ACKNOWLEDGEMENTS

I NEED to thank all my London staff for their tremendous support and back-up given during the frantic months preparing this book, and especially Veronique Henderson for her organisational and creative input with photography and design; Sue Abbott for her critical editing; and Liz Baker for firefighting. Trevor Castleton, my joint MD, ran the company so smoothly in my absences that I might be tempted to write more in the future.

Jeff Grant of Robert Half Associates conducted vital research on my behalf, to prove that image is so important to today's decision-makers.

Angie Michaels kept me alert on changes in US corporate image policies and practices and remains a dear friend as well as a most respected associate in image consulting.

Thanks also to Peter Heggie and all my friends at Austin Reed; Bob Ambrose, Leonard Ifayemi, Sue McAinsh and the entire team at Selfridges; Mark Binnington of Next Directory; Mr. Humbles and the colourful chaps of Turnbull & Asser; Nicholas Wheeler of Charles Tyrwhitt; Victoria Gooder of Gucci; all who so generously provided the smart clothes used throughout the book to demonstrate key points.

Special thanks to our handsome models: Justin Harris, Nick Hearn, Steve Hood, Lawrence Butler, Mark Fish, Alf Rodenby and Daniel Farmer.

Designer Paul Saunders gives his best to all my books, and this one is no exception.

To Judy Piatkus, Gill Cormode and Philip Cotterell of Piatkus Books I am grateful for their recognising the merit of my material, and to Heather Rocklin for getting it into shape.

INTRODUCTION

THIS is a personal book: it is for and about **you** and how you present yourself every day in your working life. It is for men in large corporations as well as those in small start-up enterprises and it attempts to cross national and cultural boundaries, being relevant for both profit-making and non-profit sectors.

You may well ask what qualifies me to write such a book. I am an image consultant but also a business manager, strategic planner, speaker and trainer. This is career number three for me, the previous ones having been in government (US) and in management consulting. I have managed budgets of $50 million, and directed staff numbering over 100. But I am most proud of building a successful international organisation from scratch, and directing a network of 1,000 consultants. I share my background not to boast but to show that in addition to acting as a consultant to many organisations (among them, Barclays Bank, Marriott Hotels, Mercury Communications, Prudential Insurance, Marks & Spencer and ICI), I have had personal experience of working in business and understand first-hand the challenges in, and importance of, getting one's image right.

In the course of my work as an image consultant I have met many men whose fathers weren't professional or 'white-collar' and, in consequence, had a difficult time figuring out how to dress and behave in business. They had no role model to guide them and, unless fortunate enough to pick up the signals of other successful men, found themselves stymied in their careers because they didn't look or act the part.

Coming to Britain and Europe in the early 1980s, I recognised the potential of offering a new service – image consulting – which had started in the States a few years previously. The name was a problem – in my target countries not only was 'image consultant' not heard of before but, worse still, it was so un-European. Americans might be mad keen on self-improvement but Europeans were loathe to admit that they might be underconfident about anything. My battle, needless to say, was uphill.

That was 10 years ago. Over those years I and my team have studied everything we could on design, fashion, tailoring, colour. We have joined forces with top communications specialists, sought advice from management gurus and behavioural psychologists, and researched the impact of various images and approaches in different cultures, on men and women. Everything from the art of tailoring to presentation skills has been mastered and reworked in ways that answered what we knew were the needs of real business people.

Today we are sought by political parties as well as blue-chip companies for advice. Many men now consider a session with an image consultant no stranger than going to a health farm for a welcome retreat. Perhaps as a result of such beneficial experiences many are also now ready to accept that having a facial is not the prerogative of women – and brings positive results for men also.

BEING DONE OVER

When a man visits CMB for an image consultation you can imagine his trepidation. Talk about laying yourself on the line! But this natural reserve disappears as we first discuss the image of his organisation and how colleagues dress. In no time, any personal insecurities begin to surface. 'I look too young (or too old).' 'I have a miserable shape and can never get anything to look smart on me.' 'My wife used to buy everything for me but now that we are divorced, I'm lost.' 'I feel that when I travel abroad on business I look scruffy and old fashioned.' 'My boss is put off by my appearance – it's so different from his. But, frankly, I don't want to look as boring as he does.'

Every CMB consultation is unique, because each client is given individual attention. But the structure of the session is basically the same, covering an assessment of his present image and advising him on his best colours, styles of suits, how to combine suits, shirts and ties with confidence, and tips for developing a wardrobe within a budget as well as how to shop most effectively. All this is done considering his particular position, circumstances and lifestyle.

You are Your Most Important Asset

A poor image is self-defeating; it gets in the way of you projecting your true qualities and abilities. Many men – and women – *wish* this wasn't the case, that we should all be assessed only on our achievements not on any additional, *superficial* factor, such as appearance. But *you* are an essential tool in communicating your ideas. How you are packaged speaks volumes about how you value yourself and respect others, about your sense of quality, creativity and professionalism.

Our guidance often results in profound change. Colleagues and customers applaud the change not knowing quite what happened to the man, just realising that something positive definitely has happened. For, as you will learn in this book, a successful image is not about people noticing your snappy suits or ties, or being dazzled by your watch. It is about people noticing you first, almost unable to remember later what you were wearing but having the impression that you looked professional, attractive and *successful*.

YOUR REFERENCE BOOK ON IMAGE

My clients and their enthusiastic feedback inspired me to write this book about what it takes to present your best. I hope that, in its turn, it will inspire you.

After a seminar or personal consultation most men take two or three key recommendations on board immediately. They might begin wearing better colours, try new eyeglasses or get a more flattering hairstyle. They win compliments from colleagues, and reinforcement from clients and other contacts, which spurs them to go further, to learn even more about making the most of themselves. Their questions become deeper, more specialised. They say they need a 'reference book on image' to turn to when a new situation arises – like a trip abroad or being interviewed on television – or to help them prepare for a career move. Here it is, for them and **you**.

For Men Only

Although I enjoy doing large presentations on image for mixed audiences of men and women, rarely will I advise them about their personal image together. This is because many men – and women – feel a certain reservation about discussing their image problems in mixed groups, and that makes it difficult to get down to the nitty-gritty.

This book covers many *sensitive* topics like hairy nostrils, stained teeth, bad breath, receding hair, fluctuating waistlines, even make-up – which you'll need to learn about for some presentations and television interviews. My language is often very direct but, from experience of working with men for many years, I know this is what you want and what you respond to best.

The Critical Boss

The route taken by many bosses who are faced with an employee with a bad image, is to call him in and subject him to an embarrassing critique. The employee then has to live with facing the boss always mindful of the humiliating experience. The situation is made even more stressful by the fact that few bosses know how to advise, how to help the troubled employee make the necessary changes. That's where an image consultant comes in and where this book will be a useful reference tool – as much for managers and personnel directors responsible for guiding staff on appropriate dress and good personal presentation as for the employee.

YOUR COMPLETE PRESENTATION GUIDE

This book explains why *you* are the message in business and public life, and how others read you. Whatever your image is today, and no matter how well it may have worked for you thus far in your career, it might not be right for you tomorrow, to project what's needed to help you succeed in new areas.

In the following chapters, you'll decide what qualities you want to project and audit your current image to see how you measure up. You will be encouraged to assess the correlation between your company or organisation's image and your own personal image. Read how and why some companies have used image training as a way to realign management objectives and to help men prepare for new challenges in their careers.

You will see what it takes to develop an image that suits your present position, your lifestyle and your personality. Don't fear arbitrary prescriptions. There is no one winning formula: 'Buy this suit, shirt and tie in these colours and this style and you'll look right.' It's not that simple but neither is it difficult. The key will be to identify what is unique about yourself first – your own natural colouring, build and personality – and then to see which of the many options for creating a positive image appeals to you most. You will also want to be aware of the sometimes subtle, but often profound, differences between sectors and across national boundaries and how to adapt your image when necessary.

The foibles of men's body shapes are laid bare, not to poke fun but to teach you some simple but effective tricks to camouflage your problems and accentuate your assets. You'll discover a colour palette to make wardrobe co-ordination an easy task, and to make you look healthy and credible. You will focus on fabrics, cuts and styles that will be both comfortable and effective. The details of good image – your accessories, your grooming, even your underwear – are equal in importance to the big items such as your suits.

Find out how your present image and wardrobe measure up and what should top your next shopping list.

Your grooming provides the polish; your fitness provides the energy. Why short-change yourself by being well-groomed but unfit, or in-shape but badly dressed?

The modulation of your voice accounts for 38 per cent of the impact you make on others. How well-tuned is yours? Find out if you need to improve your voice in order to ensure that more people listen to you – and are impressed with what you say.

Across the table, in meetings and interviews, your image is under the spotlight. Many careers have been made or side-tracked simply due to the manner in which individuals have handled themselves in meetings and the signals they projected.

Every time you get up to speak you are presenting yourself. Learn how to stage manage your own success.

Television is no longer the purview solely of Senior Executives, so in the following pages you can find out how to prepare for your initiation into the public eye. Discover how to present yourself on camera with confidence, from how to do your own make-up, what to wear, how to sit, to how to handle the interview itself.

As the world gets smaller – or more accessible – and many of us now travel more extensively in our jobs, you'll also learn how to prepare for a business trip abroad. I'll help you think through the challenge of creating a positive impression on foreigners – the key being to think of them first.

So let's get started, with the shared aim to ensure that **your** image projects the best about **you**.

CHAPTER 1

YOU ARE THE MESSAGE

STOP for a minute and ask yourself why you have bought this book? Perhaps a friend recommended it or maybe you were intrigued after flipping through. Somewhere in you lurks questions about your personal image and the impact it is having on your career. How do you think you present yourself to the world? How do you think others judge you, particularly those who don't know you well or who are meeting you for the first time? What do you want to project to others; which qualities do you admire and would like others to identify in you?

The following is a non-exhaustive list of adjectives, some of which might describe you. Which three of them do you feel are most important for other people to recognise in you?

• Co-operative	• Mature	• Youthful
• Attractive	• Friendly	• Urbane
• Kind	• Professional	• Capable
• Clever	• Dynamic	• Efficient
• Successful	• Disciplined	• Powerful
• Reliable	• Creative	• Ambitious
• Hard-working	• Organised	• Effective

Jot down the three key words you think, or would like to, describe yourself. Ask yourself how apparent these are to others in your professional life, when assessing you.

Imagine yourself having coffee with a colleague at a café near the office. In comes the Managing Director of a competitive company for whom your colleague used to work. He joins you both for a few minutes. In that brief time, what impression do you think you made? If we asked him to use three adjectives to describe you, would they be the ones you've jotted down? If you want to look *clever* and *creative* how do you project that in a few minutes over coffee without being obnoxious and monopolising the conversation? How can others sense that you are *reliable* or *efficient* without a full report from your supervisor? How can you look *successful*, or potentially so, without bragging about your achievements?

The answer is: by your projected image: your dress, your grooming, your voice and your behaviour tell people who you are even before they have established personal contact with you. We all size each other up, make judgements about each other's values, backgrounds and capabilities within minutes of meeting. If you dress very safely without much flair, is there any chance that people will think you are *creative*? If your voice is hesitant, your eye contact fleeting, will you be dismissed as underconfident rather than *successful*? If your nails are bitten to the quick, do you project being a *disciplined* professional? If you drink fizzy Cola at 10:00 a.m., do you look *mature* and *urbane*? How you look, how you speak, how you comport yourself all send out vital messages to say what you are about, how successful you are and, to some extent, what you have the potential to become.

IT TAKES INTEGRITY

You may already be bristling. As you read how important are your clothes, your behaviour and, for heaven's sake, even what you drink, you may be ready to dismiss this advice as superficial, even ridiculous. Not so – don't think for a minute that I am suggesting that you can learn a few tricks and fool everyone that you are someone that you are not.

Your image needs to have integrity if it is going to work. What you project should be what you are about; if you can't fulfil expectations your image will collapse around you. But this does not mean that if you know you have shortcomings they can't be overcome. If you are terrified of speaking in front of people, you *can* learn how to deal with the stress, how to prepare and deliver a good presentation. If your dress is indifferent, you *can* learn how to dress better, look smarter. If your parents didn't teach you the finer points of table etiquette, it is *not* too late to learn how to navigate your way through a five-course meal in a five-star restaurant.

A successful image makes the most of who you are, and gives you the confidence to be yourself in any situation.

Who Says So

You will be reassured to learn that I am not the only advocate of the importance of a good personal image to your career prospects. Research today shows that image makes or breaks your chances of getting a job, let alone getting ahead.

Chief Executive Officers, Personnel and Managing Directors in America and Europe concur that to hope for serious consideration for a job you must look the part. Robert Half Associates, on behalf of CMB, surveyed 300 top UK Financial and Personnel Directors in June 1992. In the UK, 93 per cent of top decision-makers agreed that personal presentation was the key factor in gaining employment. The more senior the executive, the more he said image was vital to job success and advancement. In today's highly competitive job market just being qualified, better still experienced, simply isn't enough to get the job you want. Employers are looking for more.

In a 1990 survey of Chief Executive Officers and Personnel Directors of Fortune 1000 companies, researchers from the School of Management at Syracuse University (Herbert Knoll and Clint Tankersley), found that not only did 96 per cent agree on the importance of personal presentation, but also that a successful image was most important in highly visible jobs like Sales and Marketing, followed by Human Resources, Finance and Accounting. Even for those not in the 'front-line' in jobs like research and development, image was important for career advancement. But few companies provide image training, despite 86 per cent of them agreeing that they could benefit from projecting a better corporate image to their clients.

Other interesting findings from the Knoll and Tankersley study include:

- Communication skills (writing, presentation skills, clear articulation) were considered the most important contributors to a positive image.
  Next in importance was all aspects of personal presentation – grooming (that is, personal hygiene details ... skin, hair and fingernails), appearance (over-all image ... body shape, fitness, dress), and manners.

- Managing and Personnel Directors considered a good image more important than holding a postgraduate degree!

- All respondents from these top companies believed that the corporate image had a direct impact on their profitability.

THE WAY YOU SEE YOURSELF

Your image affects not only how others perceive you but, equally important, how you perceive yourself. When you look good you feel more confident, you value yourself more and enjoy reinforcement from others. On days you don't bother about your appearance, you are more likely to retreat from opportunities to stand out, and to shine.

Your image affects your performance. If you look good you get more recognition from others – because you look the part. Think about when you receive positive recognition at work . . . 'great presentation', 'you handled that situation well', 'you're looking fit', and so on. Doesn't it make you feel great? If you have performed well, have met expectations or better still surpassed them, don't you want to keep it up, to deliver more of the same?

The reinforcement process of a positive self-image is cyclical. A better image leads to improved self-esteem, which gives you more confidence, which encourages your performance, that earns you more recognition which returns to bolster your self-esteem. It goes on and on.

In our work as image consultants, all too often we see the reverse process at work. Perfectly capable, talented and hard-working people are stymied in their careers because their poor self-image and low self-esteem inhibits them from expressing themselves and getting the recognition they deserve. A negative image – dressing badly, poor grooming, being unfit, underconfident behaviour, lacking presence – can actually lead to a deterioration in performance and, in some instances, almost to paranoia.

So your appearance affects you just as much as it affects others with whom you live, work and meet every day. What gets in the way of your feeling completely confident in yourself? What jibes have you taken from friends or colleagues about your dress, weight, skin, hair that have hurt you in the past? Have you tried to improve your image, since starting your career? If not, can you afford to pull down the shutters and not deal with the barriers to your own success?

Your Image Audit

This book presents an opportunity for you to take a long, hard look at yourself and to be honest about what aspects of your image are letting you down in your career. In the following chapters, we will focus on your appearance and how you might make more of yourself but, before we get down to the basics, let's see which aspects of your image you are satisfied with and where you know you need help. For each of the listed image factors on page 18, tick how you rate yourself.

Image Factor	A Liability	On a par with peers	Above Average	First-rate
Quality of voice	☐	☐	☐	☐
Communication skills (written & verbal)	☐	☐	☐	☐
Presentation skills	☐	☐	☐	☐
Social skills	☐	☐	☐	☐
Table manners	☐	☐	☐	☐
Eye-contact	☐	☐	☐	☐
Handshake	☐	☐	☐	☐
Posture	☐	☐	☐	☐
Fitness	☐	☐	☐	☐
Grooming (hair, skin, hands, etc.)	☐	☐	☐	☐
Dress/personal style	☐	☐	☐	☐
Manners	☐	☐	☐	☐

Give yourself 3 points for every factor you have judged to be *first rate*, 2 points for every one you consider to be *above average;* and 1 point for every one where you are *on par with your peers*. Obviously, you earn no points for your self-judged liabilities.

- If you scored **fewer than 8** points, your image is killing you. How you have lasted in your job is a mystery.

- If you scored between **9 and 12** points, you are Mr Average, who offends few but scores little with people who count in your career – your current and future employers.

- If you gave yourself **13 to 24** points, you show some promise but present an inconsistent image – good in some aspects, weak in others.

- If you scored **25 to 36** points, you know that your image is important and have no doubt worked on improving yourself. You may have had the advantage of growing up with parents who taught you manners and dining etiquette, and who instilled an appreciation of being well-dressed. But other aspects you have had to learn either through special training, reading, or by being observant of others. Well done.

However you scored, you will now have a much clearer idea of any shortcomings. And you are already better placed to deal with them. You deserve to have a first-rate image, one that presents you in your best light, shows respect and appreciation of others and, most important, gives you the confidence to be yourself. That is what this book is about – making the most of who you are and learning to avoid sending out the wrong signals with a poor image in your professional life.

FINE-TUNING THROUGHOUT YOUR CAREER

Like everything in life, we keep learning from experience. Think about a meeting – business or social – that went disastrously wrong. Maybe you were ill-prepared, arrived too late or too early. Perhaps you misunderstood the event and came over-dressed or under-dressed. Or, maybe your nerves got the better of you and you babbled on knowing that you were boring everyone but unable to stop. Whatever went wrong, be comforted in knowing that we have all had such experiences – and we can learn from them.

Be aware of the need to develop your image throughout your career, that what works at one level, in one business, in one culture might not be appropriate or successful in another. The shrewdest businessman assesses the intangible nature of new and different environments and makes the necessary adjustments not merely to fit in – but to succeed.

No matter what stage you are at in your career you can benefit from reading on. You've audited your image at the beginning of this chapter, and anything you ticked as a *Liability* or simply *On a Par with Peers* is not going to help you progress in your career. Those are your priorities for sorting out, and now is the moment to start to put them right.

CHAPTER 2

THE INDUSTRY, THE IMAGE

AS WE have already noted, the business of image is integral to every organisation, whether a multi-national conglomerate or a single-issue, non-profit group. An image or corporate identity must be formed and projected before any trader can hope to sell his products or services. Without one he has difficulty projecting what his business is all about, what it offers and where it is going.

When you think of Corporate Image, what springs to mind? Consider some of the best-known household names like Sony, Coca-Cola, Virgin, McDonald's and Perrier. You can visualise their branding . . . McDonald's golden arches; the red and white Coke cans. And their distinctive logos often incorporate simple lettering which is understood in any language, and in most cultures, making it easy for customers to identify them on the high street, in the supermarket, in the trade directories, and the logo's strength and success also reminds the individual organisation of what it stands for and where it fits in its competitive market.

Apart from the important corporate logo there are many other image statements . . . the company brochures, its advertising, the packaging of its products, its offices, factories and headquarters and, in some companies, staff uniforms. All of these combine to produce a composite image of the company. But, too often, this is where corporate image planning, thought and investment stops, just short of the company's most important assets – its people.

YOUR CORPORATE IMAGE

Think of the buzz words used to describe your company or organisation. Maybe you have played a part in developing some of the corporate communication materials, the brochures or advertising. Or possibly you train new personnel in the corporate culture. What is your company trying to project to the outside world? Write down the first five adjectives that spring to mind.

When I ask this question in my seminars, after about 10 seconds out come the predictable, and relevant, responses: *professional, friendly, successful, international, creative, reliable, traditional, responsive, forward-thinking*, are among the most common proffered, regardless of the company or the product. If these are the adjectives being projected by many companies, via their advertising and other forms of communication about themselves, the organisations must ask themselves if all their staff – from the receptionists and customer service people to the technical and quality control specialists, the sales and marketing teams, and yes – the top management – project these qualities as well.

If a company says that its products are top *quality* but its service reps/sales-men dress in shabby, ill-fitting suits, will the claim be as believable as it would be if those same reps were well-groomed and more presentable? If your services really are *professional* but the trainer you send to conduct a pilot course doesn't wear a suit, will you have the authority you hoped for with that client? If you say that your bank is really *friendly*, that is, that customers can come in and discuss their problems with your staff yet most of the latter are dressed like policemen in navy suits and white shirts, do you think that invites people to share their problems and feel they are getting a friendly welcome? You want to project that you are a *creative* and *forward-thinking*

You should reflect your company's image

company yet the men all look clones, each wearing a forgettable suit and tie. Will the great *tradition* of your company come across if your receptionist wears jeans? Is your claim of *reliability* believable if your marketing managers look too trendy?

SYNERGY IS THE GOAL

Every organisation should aim for a correlation between the corporate image and the personal image of its staff, who should look to reinforce the values the company is aiming to project through all its other communications. Standards for personal image should be cultivated throughout the organisation, with guidelines to help staff appreciate what's needed to keep existing customers and to win new ones, to project all the corporate goals favourably.

When clients meet your company's representatives they should be impressed by the qualities of those representatives. That is not to say that staff must dress in a really high-powered style, sporting slick suits and snappy brief-cases. They always need to be dressed appropriately for the industry and for the clients. In today's highly competitive world, when companies produce equally good services or products, keep books with the same attention to detail, can service computer systems as efficiently as countless others, etc., it comes down to the staff making the difference – they can add value to both the image and the reality of the organisation's purpose and capabilities.

Don't imagine, however, that just by smartening up, you'll have all that's required to gain the advantage over your competitors. You and your staff must know your stuff, be qualified and capable of sustaining any partnership with customers. But how you all look can tell your customers that your company has more, that you are what you say you are when it comes to your products or services and even more so when it comes to your people.

Many companies have turned to CMB for advice on how their staff could make a better impression on clients and customers. Some are mainly concerned with projecting a better image internally and ask us to help redefine the corporate image in terms of how the staff dress. More often, there's a catalyst for change: a new management team comes in; a company wants to expand its export markets; or a department gets reorganised; companies and corporate cultures merge; or perhaps the turnover of good staff is too high.

The following are a few case studies of organisations going through a transition who considered that the image of their staff needed some improvement.

1: GOING PRIVATE

In the last few years several of Britain's utility services previously managed in the public sector were privatised. This generated great upheaval in many of the regional utility organisations. Most engaged management consultants to assess their systems and efficiency. Several teams were told to approach CMB for advice on how to *look* more efficient and businesslike even before the new systems were put into place.

The Contracting Manager at one of the utility boards, after attending a presentation at the Confederation of British Industry on Managing Your Image, spoke to me of his concern about how he and his management team would cope with having to report to a new Board of Directors in the private sector rather than to civil servants. His concerns mirrored those throughout the industry with whom we had already designed seminars and executive coaching programmes.

I was invited to meet the management team who were in varying degrees anxious about what 'going private' would mean. They understood clearly enough that they would be 'profit-driven' instead of 'service-driven', as they were when a publicly-owned utility. It was more the intangible side of the transformation that concerned them: dealing with customers, dealing with a board, and how they should present themselves. They wanted to know how they could become more like real businessmen than the public servants they had been for so long.

Over lunch when we discussed their worries and the demands of the privatisation, I was bemused at where we ate and how *they* ate. We were in a small, sterile room which they used when entertaining customers, particularly local businessmen. It was clean and presentable but devoid of any colour or atmosphere. Both the tablecloth and napkins were made of paper, the placemats were photos of equipment used in the industry and the centrepiece consisted of an orange plastic floral display, steel salt and pepper shakers, and a bowl of toothpicks.

The forgettable lunch was served by two canteen ladies who had been borrowed for the occasion. They wore their regulation kitchen uniforms, were motherly rather than smart, and one lady consistently served from the wrong side.

To complete the picture, this friendly, down-to-earth management team had manners more appropriate for the pub than for a corporate dining room or restaurant. They reached for bread across their neighbour's plate, spoke with their mouths full and didn't once let go of their cutlery until they had scooped up the final portions on their plates.

I soaked up the atmosphere as well as their behaviour, then let them have it over coffee. If they intended to operate like successful businessmen they had to look and act the part. This needed not only a seminar on improving their dress, which was nondescript and dated, but also to have a session on dining etiquette. The hospitality room was bad enough, but coupled with their manners, a recipe for disaster, rather than sufficient to impress their customers or their new board of respected business leaders.

To their credit, they took my frank assessment of their images and etiquette constructively, absorbing all the advice offered. After a tough seminar on what they needed to change in their appearance, most went out and bought their completely new recommended look. I also made suggestions for adding a touch of 'class' to the formerly bleak decor of the corporate dining room, and menus that were more palatable. I also recommended hiring professional caterers to serve hospitality meals.

We had a lesson in etiquette over a lunch at which they shared their insecurity about which utensil to use when, how to tackle certain foods and how to conduct business over lunch. The point of learning the rules of etiquette is then being able to relax over a meal, to enjoy yourself while putting your guests at ease and to conduct the necessary business at hand.

Months later I was invited back for 'an inspection', prior to an important board visit. The men looked terrific, all individual in their new suits and ties, and beautifully groomed. The Head of Finance told me that he was getting a completely different reception from business clients, thanks to his new look, which gave him greater confidence than he'd ever had before.

I coached each man through his presentation for the board, editing most of them down to half of what they had intended to say and urging them to use only an outline rather than to speak from a full text, to project more competence and self-confidence.

These men, in mid-career, had to undergo a significant image transformation in order to succeed in their new business environment. Because they did, they are more confident in handling their jobs and new challenges brought about with privatisation. They were so enthusiastic about the results that they adopted a CMB dress code for their entire organisation.

2: GROOMING FOR HIGH EXPOSURE

Sometimes the 'best and the brightest' in an organisation are the least presentable. This happened to be the case when we were called in to a major financial institution to advise top managers on their image.

Among this enthusiastic group of about a dozen was a quiet, but well-spoken fellow who had just been designated to handle a company-wide Quality Initiative which needed selling to both staff and the industry. Although all the participants received the requisite personal critique and

It's the small things like your choice of tie that register where you are in your career

guidance on image, I particularly homed in on this manager because he projected all the wrong things when his job was to project quality.

Under pressure to design the new Quality programme, John had worked long hours, eating poorly and not getting enough exercise, which meant he had put on a substantial amount of weight. His suits no longer fitted, he looked untidy, and the whole image shouted 'failure', although he was to mastermind the programme. His management wanted to send him out to industrial conferences, to handle large client presentations, which he was very able to do in substance, but he was doomed to fail before he set off due to an image that contradicted his message.

After the seminar, he took the suggestion that we meet in London for a shopping trip to get together the requisite clothes for his important forthcoming meetings and presentations. Like most achievers, John was receptive to criticism and took all my suggestions to heart, including the most sensitive and difficult one of losing weight and getting back his old fitness. This will take about a year to achieve on a sensible – not crash – diet. Meanwhile he needed a few good suits to make him look both slimmer and more successful. Everything required fine-tuning, the fit of suits and shirts as well as the grooming, with a better haircut to make the most of his fine, thinning, mane.

John reported back that everyone commented on how much better he looked. In his new suits, they thought he had lost weight even before he started the diet in earnest. Because previously his suits were so uncomfortable, he rarely wore a jacket around the office. 'Now I always wear one and they are hopping to attention. I can't believe what a difference it makes.'

John is typical of countless talented and hardworking professionals who are the backbone of many organisations. But because their image lets them down they risk being prevented from going any further. John knew this was a 'make or break' point in his career, and he was determined to make it. He was big enough, figuratively, to say 'help' and to take professional advice designed to improve his condition. Today, there is no stopping him.

His company was so impressed by John's new image that it requested image seminars for its staff around the country involved with the Quality Initiative. This training has had a catalytic effect, with staff reinforcing the changes in each other, and the improved appearance of the teams has had a positive effect on their attitude to work.

3: MATCHING IMAGE AND REALITY

When a new Managing Director takes over, often intangible things like the image of the staff become major concerns, an irritation that can get in the way of doing business. This was exactly what happened within months of a dour, dry-witted Scot taking over the helm of a prestigious motor group.

In 1990, when the new MD Angus came on board, this luxury car distributorship was the recognised market leader in Great Britain, dealing only with top of the line models like Rolls-Royce, Jaguar, Land Rover and Mercedes Benz. But the recession was beginning to loom and the new MD knew that they couldn't rest on their fine reputation, that the organisation had to be competitive in every way. He also recognised that the company was not competitive in terms of its staff. They were capable at selling cars all right but they had the wrong image for this specialised market. Angus is dapper, the antithesis of what you imagine a car dealer to look like. He wears dark pin-stripe suits, of the finest quality and is impeccably groomed.

His difficulty was that his top distributors had images ranging from those of subservient shop assistants to slick 'spivs'. Others dressed less well than their staff, which he felt created morale problems in the showroom. If the staff made an effort to look good, why shouldn't the boss who earned much more?

The suggestion that the men should smarten up, proffered by Angus at one of his first management meetings, was greeted with derision. He later tried tactful one-to-one sessions urging managers to 'do something', and it emerged that the real problem was that they didn't know what to do, nor could Angus advise them specifically about what changes to make. He contacted us at CMB.

In this instance, I felt that the issue of image could best be dealt with as a team. I could take the heat off Angus if they agreed as a group what image they should adopt for the company. I could then guide each of them on specific changes required to achieve the desired end result.

Getting agreement on what image they as dealers in luxury cars should have, proved more difficult than we imagined. Some felt that they were there to serve their wealthy customers and that a service image should not be flashy or better than that of the customers. Others felt they should look as wonderful as their products, be proud to stand out. The only trouble was that they saw this as licence to wear loud ties, trendy suits and slick hair styles – the antithesis of what Angus wanted to project.

After much discussion, we agreed that first and foremost the managers needed to look professional, which meant navy or grey suits, not green or purple ones. Next, they needed to project success, by wearing good quality suits, significantly better than most were wearing at the time. And finally, they wanted to be as individual as their products, which meant that they should not all dress in the same way.

The management team concurred that they had to set the standard for their own junior salesmen, that they had to look the part first if they expected their staff to conform to the new corporate image.

Over the next months, each manager was taken on a shopping trip to choose the supplementary items needed to boost his existing wardrobe and measure up to our new definition. Some needed suits, shirts, ties, shoes – the works. Others just needed a more respectable hairstyle or more interesting ties. One, whom I had told at the seminar that he looked 10 years older than he was, resumed running and lost two stone in a matter of a few months, improving both his image and his energy level.

After six months, Angus had a much improved team of Sales Managers and a good rapport built on a management style that developed consensus and provided firm leadership.

WHAT IMAGE WORKS BEST?

In these case histories I described very different organisations with very different cultures. To understand better what some of these different images looked like, here are some guidelines I use for different organisations.

Exceptions to the Rule

An organisation's size greatly influences the guidelines for personal image of the employees. Large companies, with more formal systems for communication and management hierarchy, are most comfortable and reassured by the trappings of professionalism – the formal business suit, good grooming and appropriate accessories.

There are exceptions to this, however, such as those companies whose organic growth initially came from a different business culture. Two notable examples familiar to many are Anita Roddick's Body Shop and Richard Branson's former Virgin Group (now, of course, he heads Virgin Atlantic). Highly successful business people, both Roddick and Branson are iconoclastic; they challenge many traditional business values and practices. They don't have to play by the rules; they have made it in spite of them. With their success and leadership they might even help to relax standards of business dress. But until their 'devil may care', anti-establishment images are accepted by more companies you are advised to follow the guidelines in this book, which are based on experience and research of what works to get ahead in your career. Developing a good image to project your best is for 99.9 per cent of people in 99.9 per cent of professional organisations and businesses.

Small companies form and prosper off the backs of a few dedicated people willing to wear many hats. Because everyone is expected to 'muck in' as needed, the image of employees needs to be easier, less severe than in larger organisations. The MD will get the extra effort from his staff if they recognise that he is 'one of them' in a sense, that the top person is approachable as well as being 'in charge'. Hence, rather than the suit every day, the MD could wear a sports-jacket and toning trousers. He can also be seen around the office in his shirt sleeves, without losing whatever authority is necessary. But he should wear a jacket for meetings, particularly with outside contacts.

Urban Cowboys or Rural Slickers?

The BBC once asked if I would advise a paint manufacturing company just outside Manchester in the North of England. I was one of a group of 'New Age' management consultants put in touch with this company, to see what good, if any, we could do to improve their business.

This medium-size family-owned company with an £8 million annual turnover, prided itself on being friendly and approachable. Only the Managing Director wore a suit. His brother, the Marketing and Sales Director, wore short-sleeved shirts and trainers. The Sales Reps wore sports jackets and trousers. The casual image of this company had worked for over 50 years, but competition was nipping at its heels. They wanted to know if they really required smartening up. The Managing Director and the Marketing Director had opposing views, which were reflected in their own images.

Their customers were mainly industrial companies based in rural areas or outside main city centres. An industrial site is quite unlike a modern business complex of offices. Often heavy-duty work gets done and on equipment significantly larger than a desktop computer or photocopier. Smart suits are not only impractical, in that they are not meant to be subjected to heavy-duty wear on industrial sites, but they are also off-putting. My clients had it right in principle. They needed to dress in a way calculated to make their customers feel comfortable. Jackets and trousers were fine for the sales reps, although they needed significant upgrading from what they had. But the Management team, especially the Marketing and Sales Director, had to look more like a board member – in charge, capable of taking decisions – not as if he spent half his working day on the assembly line.

Look Approachable

To look more approachable yet successful, men managing small companies or working in rural locations, should wear single-breasted suits. Today there are wonderful, easy designs in a range of colours less severe than the traditional dark navy or grey. Single-breasted jackets can be worn open, they are far more comfortable than double-breasted styles and they look more relaxed. While smart blazers or sport jackets and trousers are acceptable for sales reps visiting rural customers, management need to be more formal in their dress, especially for meetings with customers. To appear more part of the team around the plant, managers in small companies can leave off their jackets but will look more groomed, more professional in long-sleeved shirts. In warm weather, it is preferable to roll the sleeves up rather than wear short-sleeved shirts which, whatever their cost, never look successful.

Traditional or Progressive?

Rarely, when I ask people to describe their corporate image, do they include both of the above attributes – either a company sees itself as traditional or as progressive. Generally, the traditional companies have been in business for some time and are well established, while the progressive ones are often new and aiming to chip away at their more traditional competitors.

In business today, it can be risky to be exclusively *traditional* or *progressive*. Those overly concerned with a traditional image might be perceived as too stuck in their ways, not adapting to changes in the marketplace. Certain professional firms like solicitors, doctors, accountants, fall into this trap. While they want to inspire confidence in having a wealth of experience, they also need to project that they are up-to-date, aware of new innovations, services and approaches. It is a fact, also, that firms that value being and looking very progressive can worry customers that what they are selling or preaching as relevant for today might be redundant tomorrow. So projecting a balance is clearly important for any company.

Traditional firms need to shake their foundations from time to time to be sure their image is current as well as professional. Are they, for instance, still wearing boring ties when their clients – equally successful men – are expressing more personality? However, very trendy suits will get a raised-eyebrow response from your peers so stick with elegant, classic cuts and experiment more with subtle changes in colours for your suits, shirts and ties.

The younger the company the more it needs to instil confidence in its staying power. It needs to project reliability and resilience of the products, people and, especially, of the company. Hence, staff working in new, dynamic concerns are advised to be more sober and reassuring in their dress. Men might choose modest style suits in traditional colours, good quality shirts with standard collars and elegant yet current ties, avoiding the trendy, the loud or the garish ones so often sported in new, aggressive organisations.

The more progressive the company, often, the younger the staff. Young men are keen to look 'with-it', or fashionably-dressed, and often take years – vital ones in terms of career opportunities – to shape up and look professional. Trendy Doc Martens look great at the weekends but they do not finish a suit. Ear-rings might be terribly cool to your mates but are off-putting to most business men and women. Play smart and play down your youth and trendiness to make a better impression on more traditional colleagues and customers.

CHAPTER · 3

DOES YOUR IMAGE MEASURE UP?

WOMEN often complain that men have it so easy. All they have to do is put on a suit and they're considered well-dressed. But in business today, most men are aware that if they do stick to a nondescript suit 'uniform', they are not well-dressed. Look around at your office colleagues, notice other men on the train on the way to or from work, or at business dinners. You'll observe that some men look more together than others – you may not quite know what's different about their suits, shirts and ties and other accessories but the complete outfit looks more successful to you, and definitely more interesting.

Over the last decade I have had the honour of working with men in various industries, large and small. My clients are from modest as well as privileged backgrounds, from the rich and diverse cultures of Europe, the Middle and Far East as well as North America. One thing they all have in common is a desire to look their best. They might be under-confident about a new challenge that lies ahead or feel threatened after a merger in which their former corporate culture has suffered a major transformation. Whatever the catalyst, they know that their image is no longer good enough.

Perhaps you are in a similar situation. If so, this book presents an opportunity to take a long, hard look at yourself and to be honest about what aspects of your image are letting you down in your career. So let's see how your current image measures up.

Answer the following twenty questions with a 'Yes' or 'No', then look at the answers on pages 33–35. Give yourself a point for every correct answer and add up your score.

The scores are rated on page 35.

RATING YOUR IMAGE

YES NO

1. Does it matter what your underwear looks like, so long as it's clean?

2. At a first job interview would you wear a bold tie?

3. Do excess hairs between the eyebrows make you look manly?

4. When you cross your legs do you expose 2 inches (5 cms) of your least erogenous zone?

5. Your mother has given you a tie which you don't like. Do you wear it?

6. Do you buy a new suit or shirt only when the old ones wear out?

7. Do you buy shirts and ties that are pre-matched?

8. On a day when you have an important meeting, do you dress differently?

9. In the summertime, do you wear short-sleeved shirts under your suits to keep cool?

10. Do you consider a trouser press more vital than a microwave?

11. Have you worn your hair in the same style for the last 10 years?

12. Do you polish your shoes only when you notice they're looking rather scruffy?

13. Do you use disposable pens?

14. Look at your hands and finger-nails. Do you think the Chairman would be impressed with their grooming?

15. Do you hang your suits on wire hangers?

16. Do any of your shirts have single cuffs with buttons, but also handy openings for cufflinks should you choose to wear some?

17. Is your watch composed in part of plastic or does it sport brightly-coloured motifs?

18. Does your weight fluctuate but you wear your suits snug as a reminder to watch the calories?

19. You are in a job that requires lots of one-to-one contact with people. Do you take extra care to ensure your personal hygiene is first-rate?

20. Do you like to wear colourful, fun socks as a way to express your personality?

How Did You Score?

Give yourself a point for every correct answer

1. Yes. Men in shrunken Y-fronts expose the same revealing and unattractive 'panty line' as women in tight skirts. Make sure your underwear fits properly. See also Chapter Six.

2. No. The job interview requires an understated but updated classic look. Don't try to knock them over with your wittiest tie or with an aggressive colour like red. Opt for a top quality woven silk with a subtle pattern and restrained colour, such as blue. In fact, Professor Tom Porter, Oxford Polytechnic, conducted a Tie Rack survey in 1991, which showed that most Personnel Directors consider blue most appropriate for interviews. See also Chapter Seven.

3. No. Stray hairs between eyebrows make the tidiest chap look grubby. Pluck or hot wax the unsightly hairs to look more polished. See Chapter Nine.

4. No. Only Italian, French and Japanese men realise that the stretch between their ankles and shins is their least erogenous zone. Be sure to keep yours covered with mid- or over-the-calf socks. British and German men have yet to catch on to this and manage to turn-off women as well as each other every time they cross their legs. See also Chapter Seven.

5. **No.** Your tie is your most vital statement of personality, position and power. Save mum's disaster for family get-togethers. See also Chapter Seven.

6. **No.** Your wardrobe requires enough options to allow a suit to 'rest' two to three days between wearings. Shirts should be bought two or three at a time, when you buy your suits. See also Chapter Seven.

7. **No.** Learn how to co-ordinate colours, fabrics and patterns yourself. Pre-matched choices project no creativity. See also Chapter Four.

8. **Yes and no.** For an important meeting you should consider what you want to project ... and be sure your suit, shirt and tie are the right prescription. But a successful man is consistently well-dressed every day, so he always looks right whether for planned or unplanned meetings. See also Chapter Four.

9. **No.** Unless you work in the tropics with no air-conditioning, short-sleeved shirts are only for retired book-keepers. In the summer, quality cool wool suits and 100 per cent long sleeve cotton shirts that breathe provide the necessary comfort. See also Chapter Seven.

10. **Yes.** In order of priorities, before you buy a fourth suit or a microwave, invest in a trouser press. You'll recoup the investment within a year by saving expensive pressing charges at the local cleaners as well as helping your suits to last longer. See also Chapter Six.

11. **No.** No doubt your hair line and hair texture have changed in the last decade. So if you are sporting the same style, you probably are looking older than you are. Time to visit a good stylist for a newer look. See also Chapter Nine.

12. **No.** If you leave the leather of your shoes to weather the elements until they are scuffed, you are cutting the potential lifetime of your shoes. Polish after every three wearings as soon as you take them off (while they are warm – warm leather absorbs polish better). See also Chapter Seven.

13. **No.** Disposable pens are for college students and temporary secretaries. Your pen is an important accessory which should project success and style. See also Chapter Eight.

14. **Yes.** Men are very aware of each other's hands. If you are a keen gardener or DIY enthusiast see a manicurist every two weeks, or learn how to tend them yourself. See also Chapter Nine.

15. **No.** Wire hangers destroy the line of a suit. Invest in some of the solid

wooden ones designed specifically for men's suits. See also Chapters Five and Six.

16. **No.** Avoid any design that tries to do too much. Buttoned single cuffs with cufflinks are not smart. Only wear links with proper double cuffs. See also Chapter Eight.

17. **No.** Fun, plastic watches are for weekends or teeny-boppers. The scuba-diving models or mini-computers impress no one and ruin the elegance of an otherwise professional image. See also Chapter Eight.

18. **No.** Wearing clothes in a 'hopeful size' only makes you look unkempt and feel uncomfortable. If weight is a problem, and you are unlikely to have a change of lifestyle and lose it, then buy suits that fit you when you are heavy – you'll actually look slimmer. See also Chapter Ten.

19. **Yes.** Good personal hygiene is essential for every professional but if you are in regular direct contact with people it's vital to your success. Wear freshly laundered shirts daily, shower every morning and brush your teeth after lunch as well as in the morning and evening. See also Chapter Nine.

20. **No.** Fun or novelty socks project either arrogance or immaturity. For business, always complement your suits with plain, dark socks that tone with your trousers and shoes. See also Chapter Seven.

- **If you scored 15 to 20 points,** your image is quite together. You know that you need to bother every day to make a good impression and are putting in the necessary effort. This book will help you fine-tune your image and become more successful.

- **If you scored 10 to 15 points**, your image is tired. You are not projecting as well as you need to do in order to realise your capabilities fully. Time to rethink your business image and bring yourself up-to-date. This book will guide you on all aspects. Study the advice on grooming and accessories which may be your weak points.

- **If you scored under 10 points**, your present image is hurting your career prospects. Unwittingly, you are being inconsistent and sending the wrong signals to people who matter. You need to start from scratch. Follow the tips in this book that will make a Successful Image both easy to achieve and affordable.

Whatever you scored, you will find that the following chapters provide helpful advice on all of these important aspects of image and presentation.

CHAPTER · 4

YOUR BEST COLOURS

ALTHOUGH you might have an ideal image – a look you would love to achieve – you do need to be realistic and assess your own natural assets first to determine what is possible. As image consultants, we at CMB begin with what we see, what's special about you – your colouring, your build, your scale and your personality – to ensure that the advice we then give will help you to look your best. That's your goal, not to look like someone else but to look your personal best.

DISCOVER YOUR COLOURS

If I asked which shades of blue, white, green, red or pink best suited you, could you tell me with accuracy? That is, are you aware of the subtleties between a warm red (such as rust) and a cool red (such as burgundy)? Do all greens appear the same to you; can you distinguish a bright blue green from a muted yellow green? If these questions seem inane, consider yourself lucky. Many men, far more so than women, suffer from some degree of colourblindness, making the variations of intensity and undertone of colour difficult, often impossible, to appreciate.

Even if you can distinguish colours easily, consider the suits, shirts and ties in your wardrobe. Why do you have ivory as well as white shirts? Why are there ties that only go with one shirt or one suit and nothing else? If you struggle in the morning with 'mixing and matching', you can benefit from colour analysis, to select a palette of colours that makes you look your best and also ensures that your wardrobe co-ordinates easily.

Men have come to us for colour analysis in recent years because they wanted to look healthier and more interesting. But often the main reason is that they want shopping and dressing to be less of a struggle. Think of your male colleagues. Which one looks most lacking in vitality? Do you think it might be attributed to the clothes he wears, particularly his colours?

In the right colours, you look healthy – your skin looks clearer, your eyes brighter, and other people notice you first. Think for a minute about a fellow with Deep colouring, like Sylvester Stallone (see page 40). He has dark hair, strong brown eyes and an olive complexion, and he looks wonderful in crisp white shirts, dark suits and strong ties. Imagine Stallone in a light grey suit. Would he look as interesting? Or how about Paul Newman, who has Cool colouring – a degree of pink in his skin tone, blue eyes and silver-grey hair. Now it's difficult to make such a handsome man look awful but he succeeded last year when he was interviewed wearing a warm camel jacket which made his skin look blotchy, his hair mousey and those blue eyes cloudy.

On page 38 are two men wearing identical suit and shirt colours. One is a Warm type, and the other has Deep colouring. Notice how the colours that compliment the Deep man do not flatter the Warm man.

Your Dominant Colours

At CMB, we use a system of Colour Analysis which describes people as Seasonal types, each of the four Seasons also having three variations. In personal colour consultation taking about an hour, one of our trained experts assesses your colouring and 'drapes' you through a palette of 48 colour swatches to demonstrate which colours are best for you, and representing shades for your business and casual wardrobes.

Here I will present colour more simply, suggesting a DIY approach, that will give you a basic understanding of your dominant natural colouring, and show you how to use a palette of colours to your advantage. I will also give you a detailed description of what we call the Dominant Types, to help you identify your own.

Start by looking at yourself in a mirror, in natural daylight. Try it after a shower, in your 'natural' state, so you aren't influenced by your clothes. How would you describe your colouring – the combination of your hair colour, skin tone and eye colour. Don't focus on just one feature, say, your mousey brown hair, but the overall look. Would you say your colouring is **strong and deep**, like Sylvester Stallone's, or are you **fair**? If you have freckles and red or golden tones to your skin and hair you might be **warm**. By contrast, you could look **cool** like Paul Newman. If your eyes are your dominant feature, being very bright and sparkling, with contrasting hair and skin you could be a **clear** type. 'Clear' men, like Timothy Dalton (page 48), generally have darker hair and pale skin. Or, would you say that you are somewhere in

The wrong colours can make you look pale, tired and overwhelmed. That's what is happening to Steve, a Warm type, wearing a white shirt and dark navy suit. The effect is that the suit is wearing him, not the reverse

In the right colours the eye is drawn immediately to the face, just where you want it when communicating in business. Warm men look much healthier in ivory or pastel shirts, like this peach one, rather than white. Olive suits complement red hair, freckles and hazel eyes.

Justin has deep colouring. Here he has chosen a suit simply to go with his eyes. But when choosing suits you should consider the overall impact of the colour on your skintone and hair as well as your eyes. This olive suit and muted peach shirt don't give Justin the contrast he needs.

Men with strong colouring, whether Caucasian, Black or Asian, look more interesting, fresher and healthier in sharp contrasting colours. The crisp white shirt will always be their best option, although they do have others. Dark rich colours for suits, like navy, are more successful than muted or medium tones.

between all these colouring types and look kind of **dusty and muted** . . . possibly with mousey hair, brown or hazel eyes and beige or light brown skin tone, like Eric Clapton.

If you have a receding hairline or are completely bald, the overall impact of your colouring will have changed from when you had a full head of hair; the emphasis now is more on your skin tone and the colour of your eyes – your original haircolour has no influence on what colours might suit you. However, if your eyebrows are a prominent feature, do take them into account. Otherwise, a bald head means that some of the contrast or depth you once had in your colouring has gone and now it might be better to wear **muted, cool or light** colours. (Obviously, if you have black or brown skin, you still have deep colouring and probably still look best in strong colours.)

Now that you have a very basic understanding of *why* your colouring is so important when you are choosing clothes, read the descriptions of the six Dominant Types on pages 40–51 and see which one resembles you best. Then take a look at the basic palettes recommended for the different types. Don't zero-in on the one that looks most familiar, or reject a palette because it contains colours you have never worn. Read the descriptions, look at the wardrobe of colours illustrated, and try to understand the overall look of the palette and the harmony it can create with your own natural colouring, then give it a try.

For each Dominant Type you will find colour suggestions for suits, shirts and ties as well as for your casual wear. These basic colours provide a system for building a co-ordinated wardrobe. For example, the colours recommended for your shirts will work with those listed for your ties and suits. Use the palette to edit out the wrong colours from your existing wardrobe and as a guide for shopping for new clothes.

If you would like a personal set of colour swatches in your Dominant Palette, you can order them via details on page 175.

THE DEEP TYPE

Men with Deep colouring have dark hair – black, brown – or have gone 'Salt 'n pepper' as their hair goes progressively greyer. Their eyes are normally brown or a rich hazel and their skin tone ranges from beige and 'yellow', that is, Oriental, to olive, brown or black. Above all, they project strength. For these men to look their best, their healthiest, they need to choose rich to dark coloured suits, the palest shirts and the strongest ties – especially in primary tones. In the CMB System, these men would be either Deep Autumn or Deep Winter types.

EXAMPLES: Sylvester Stallone (above left), Imran Khan, John Kennedy Jnr, Julio Iglesia, Rupert Everett, Burt Reynolds, Phillip Scofield, Seve Ballesteros, Magic Johnson, Will Carling, Linford Christie (above right), Carl Lewis

You will look your sharpest in crisp white shirts rather than pastels. You should avoid light, medium-tone or muted colours in suits; strong colours are best. And your ties should always be strong, not light or insipid.

Safe Colours for Men with Deep colouring

Shirts   Pure white   Icy blue   Icy pink or peach[1]   Icy lilac   Mint

Suits   Charcoal grey (solid or weaves that are strong not light) Charcoal brown (Looking more grey than brown)   Dark navy (solid or with fine flecks or stripes in royal or red)   Deep olive

Jackets, blazers, trousers   Black   Navy   Stone   Mahogany   Olive

Ties, sportshirts, sweaters   True red   Tomato red   Terracotta Rust   Mahogany   True green   Emerald green   Pine   Olive Hot turquoise   Teal   True blue   Purple

1. For men with a cool skin tone, i.e. a blue, pink or neutral look, pink will be better. For men with Deep colouring but warmer skin, i.e. bronze or olive, peach will be more complimentary

40

THE LIGHT TYPE

Men with Light colouring are truly fair – generally blond, light grey or white hair with blue or green eyes and a pale complexion.[2] These men need to be very careful not to overwhelm their colouring by wearing very dark or dusty colours. Try to achieve balance with mid-tone shades for suits and pastel shirts rather than pure white which can drain your face of colour.

Your wardrobe can host a variety of shades, as shown, but your colours are fresh and subtle, not bold or electric.

EXAMPLES: Paul Hogan (above), Jason Donovan, Corbin Bernsen, Chris Tarrant, Adam Faith, Clive Anderson, John Thaw

In the CMB System, the Light Spring type generally has some freckles and more golden hair. He can add camel to his wardrobe. But Light Summers don't look good in browns, other than a pink-brown, because their skin is usually pinker and their hair 'cooler', that is, ash blond or grey.

Safe Colours for Men with Light Colouring

Shirts   Pastels are great as plain or solid colours for shirts but also as soft stripes on white.
Soft white   Pastel pink or peach   Pastel blue   Mint   Icy lilac
Pale yellow

Suits   Great as solids but also mixed with other shades to create an elegant look that doesn't overwhelm, as a stronger grey would.
Medium charcoal   Charcoal blue-grey   Light navy   Pewter   Taupe

Jackets, blazers, trousers   Great as solid colours or mixed with other colours in a weave, e.g. a camel and charcoal weave.
Camel or stone[3]   Light navy   Medium blue   Medium charcoal
Powder blue/denim

Ties, sportshirts, sweaters   True blue   Medium blue
Periwinkle/violet blue   Coral/warm pinks   Powder pink   Deep rose
Watermelon red   Aqua   Blue green   Emerald turquoise
Light teal blue

2. For men with cool skin tone, i.e. a blue, pink or neutral look, pastel pink will be better. For men with Light colouring but warmer skin tone, i.e. peachy, ivory or with freckles, pastel peach will be more complimentary.

3. For men with cool skin tone the stone (a mixture of grey and beige) will be better. Men with warm skin tones look best in the camel range.

THE WARM TYPE

When men of this colour type wear a dark navy suit and a white shirt they look deathly pale, as if in need of a blood transfusion. With ivory skin tone, usually freckles, red or golden tones in the hair and brown, hazel or teal blue eyes you need to wear colours with yellow, red or green undertones that compliment your warm golden looks.

EXAMPLES: Charles Dance, Mick Hucknall, Kenneth Branagh (above), Boris Becker, Prince Philip

In the CMB system these men are called Warm Springs or Warm Autumns with the former being lighter and the latter a bit deeper in colouring. Both are complimented by grey and brown mixtures for suits and their wardrobe should be a blend of golden tones from light camels and yellows to rich olives, browns and warm greys, as shown.

Safe Colours for Men with Warm Colouring

Shirts   Ivory Buff Peach Yellow Blue[4] Terracotta

Suits   Great as solids but use camel and grey-green with caution, depending on your industry and position. Also mix in weaves e.g. a brown and charcoal birdseye, a navy with rust pinstripe, etc.
Medium charcoal   Charcoal brown   Camel   Light navy   Greyed green   Olive

Jackets, blazers, trousers   Try as solid colours or mixed in weaves with other colours from your palette.
Camel   Light navy   Terracotta   Golden brown   Bronze   Teal   Jade   Aubergine

Ties, sportshirts, sweaters   Deep peach   Tomato red   Pumpkin   Rust   Terracotta   Buff   Yellow gold   Moss   Bronze   Jade   Aqua   Turquoise   Teal   Deep periwinkle/violet blue   Purple   Aubergine

4. Blue is a good shirt colour only for those Warm men with blue eyes. Avoid if you have brown or Hazel eyes.

THE COOL TYPE

Men with Cool colouring look sickly in most shades of brown, apart from a pink brown such as cocoa.

They are much more suited to the blue tones and look wonderful in traditional business shades of grey and navy. These men have beige or pinkish skin tone, ash brown, blond or grey hair and usually have blue or blue-grey eyes. Those with brown eyes and Salt 'n Pepper hair can also look good in this palette. If you think the colours are too wishy-washy, then try those recommended for the Deep type.

EXAMPLES: Bill Clinton (above), Prince Rainier, John Major, Paul Newman, Jason Connery, Terence Stamp

In CMB we have Cool Summers and Cool Winters. They both are great in colours with a blue undertone, though Cool Winters can take much stronger versions of the colours than the Summer types. There should be no hint of khaki, camel or moss tones in your wardrobe.

Safe Colours for Men with Cool Colouring

Shirts   The recommended colours can be worn as plains or used as soft stripes on a white shirt. An 'icy' colour is predominantly white with only a dash of colour.
Soft white   Icy blue   Icy pink   Icy lilac   Mint

Suits   All of the following are good colours for plain suits but also combine for good effect e.g. the Charcoal blue-grey and soft white Prince of Wales check.
Charcoal grey   Charcoal blue-grey   Navy   Cocoa

Jackets, blazers, trousers   These are great as solid colours or mixed e.g. a cocoa, rose and navy herringbone jacket.
Cocoa   Taupe   Grey blue   Charcoal   Blue red   Teal   Pine   Navy

Ties, sportshirts, sweaters   Hot pink   Deep rose   Raspberry
Blue red   Emerald turquoise   Chinese blue   Teal   Pine   True blue
Periwinkle   Plum   Purple

THE CLEAR TYPE

These men have a lot of contrast in their natural colouring. Their hair is dark or grey, skin tone light to medium, eyes very clear like jewel-tone blue or green. Men with brown eyes and darker skintone should also consider this palette if they feel the Deep colours are too strong.

Men with Clear colouring need to compliment themselves with rich, bright colours. Your suits should never look insignificant, but rather be deep with a tie in a bold primary such as red, or royal blue. Your wardrobe should provide plenty of options to develop bold contrasts of colour for your business and casual looks, as shown opposite.

EXAMPLES: Michael Douglas, Timothy Dalton (above), Luke Perry, André Agassi

There are Clear Springs and Clear Winters, the former wearing some warmer tones such as warm pink while the latter look better in cooler pinks such as icy pink for shirts.

Safe Colours for Men with Clear Colouring

Shirts   Pure white   Icy blue   Icy pink   Icy lilac   Mint

Suits   Yours are best in solids or a weave that makes a bold impression such as a very definite pin stripe.
Charcoal grey   Navy   Charcoal brown   Deep olive/pine

Jackets, blazers, trousers   Black   Navy   Charcoal brown   Royal blue   Soft white   Stone

Ties, sportshirts, sweaters   Lemon yellow   Mango   Hot pink
Deep rose   True red   Clear teal   navy   Emerald   True green
Emerald turquoise   Hot turquoise   Chinese blue   Violet
Bright periwinkle blue

THE MUTED TYPE

This palette is a bit of a misnomer, but it's the best description I can think of. Men with this colouring are really medium in tone, that is, your hair is neither dark nor light, but it does not look particularly golden either. Often, it is grey but not very silvery. Some could be described as having mousey hair. Your skin tone is neutral – neither very pale, nor golden or too dark. Your eyes are probably a soft blend of two colours, such as blue grey, hazel green, or a soft brown, yet they project strength. This colouring can bestow a certain elegance, particularly when its owner is dressed in the blended tones of the Muted palette.

EXAMPLES: Jonathan Ross, Harry Hamlin, Eric Clapton, Robert Palmer, Mick Jagger, Don Johnson, Nigel Mansell (above)

There are Muted Summers (those with blue eyes) and Muted Autumns (those with hazel green or soft brown eyes). But there are many shades that they have in common.

Safe Colours for Men with Muted Colouring

Shirts   Soft white   Pastel blue[5]   Mint   Pastel peach or pink[6]   Light lemon yellow

Suits   Your aim is for a blended look, so very dark or very light suits aren't your best. Try mid-tone colours, with flecks of colours blended monochromatically, that is, a few shades of the same colour.
Charcoal grey   Light navy   Grey green   Pewter   Taupe   Charcoal blue-grey

Jackets, blazers, trousers   Great as solids or mixed in weaves and patterns with other colours from your palette.
Pewter   Grey green   Charcoal   Taupe   Light navy   Coffee brown   Rose brown   Jade

Ties, sportshirts, sweaters   Your ties should be interesting without overwhelming your own colouring.
Pewter   Warm pink   Deep rose   Watermelon red   Tomato red   Turquoise   Teal   Amethyst   Deep periwinkle   Purple

5. Men with muted colouring who also have blue eyes can wear the pastel blue shirt most effectively. If your eyes are Hazel or brown, a blue shirt is not particularly attractive.

6. The Muted types with blue eyes should wear the pink shirts, while those with brown or Hazel green eyes are better in peach tone shirts.

CHAPTER 5

BODY BASICS

TIME now to consider you body type – how you are built – in order to appreciate which styles of clothes, which fabrics, weaves, patterns etc. will be most complimentary to you. Women usually have a finely-honed appreciation of the variations in the female body shape. But men often only think in terms of Short, Regular or Long, Extra Large, Large, Medium or Small. To be a smart shopper and to look your best you need to consider three factors about your build when selecting clothes.

- **Body shape**
- **Proportion**
- **Height/scale**

YOUR BODY SHAPE

Take a look at the four body shapes described and illustrated below and on pages 53–4. Which one seems most like yours? You might not be an exact match for any one shape, because there are many subtle variations, but you should find that one applies to you more so than any of the other three. For each, I give some ideas for suits that will be most flattering, and more details appear on pages 56–7 and in Chapter six.

The Inverted Triangle Body

These are the men we see in magazines and at the health clubs. Broad shouldered and narrow hipped, they can be muscular versions like Sylvester

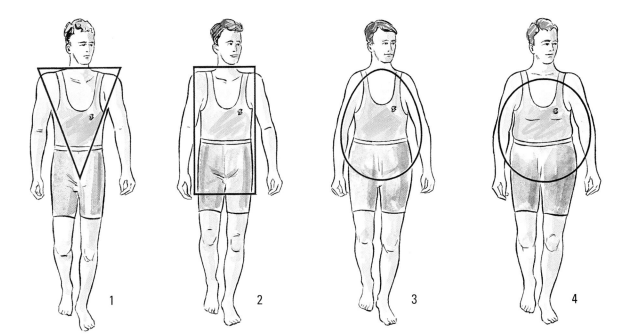

The four basic body
shapes:
1 The Inverted Triangle
2 The Straight Body
3 The Pear-shaped Body
4 The Apple-shaped Body

Stallone or, lean versions, like Jeremy Irons. They have a good choice in clothes but as their build is sharp and dramatic they look their best in European cut suits which emphasise their natural silhouette. If you have this body type, beware of selecting exaggerated designs with shoulders that are very broad, that is, even wider than yours are naturally, as they can make you look a little severe and overwhelming. Unstructured, loose-fitting jackets are fine for the weekends but avoid shapeless suits during the week.

Your trousers can be quite neat – slim cut with little pleating – or try the more fashion-forward pleated styles which look great if you have narrow hips and a flat bottom.

Your Sharp look means that loose weaves in suits won't look as interesting as really tightly woven materials which keep the sharp silhouette of the suit. Complement your angular look with crisp cotton shirts and traditional or cutaway collars rather than the softer Oxford cloth and button-down styles which would 'break down' your look. The same applies when choosing your ties – tightly woven silks, even ones with a slight satin finish, will be preferable to softer fabrics (such as woollen or cotton/silk blends).

The Straight Body

This is you, if your shoulders and hips are pretty much in line so that the silhouette, or outline of your body is a sort of rectangle. A trim version of the Straight Body type is U.S. Vice-President Al Gore. His boss, President Bill Clinton, is a more portly version. If you are tall, the European cut suit (page 60) will be a good option as it can create an illusion of broader shoulders and project a slightly more dramatic image. If you are average to short in height the Modified European cut (page 61) or the British cut (page 59) will be wonderful on you.

For trousers, you have as much choice as the previous body type inasmuch as trousers with negligible pleating or quite generous pleating can be considered. Assess the effect of the trousers without your jacket on to be sure which style is most flattering. If your bottom is broad, some pleating will be more comfortable and allow you more freedom of movement when seated.

For shirts and collars, you, too, like the Inverted Triangle, will look most striking in a traditional business shirt of poplin fabric and with a standard collar. Unless your neck is short and/or thick the Oxford cloth and button-down is not recommended.

The Pear-Shaped Body

Don't feel like a feather-weight because you've got narrow shoulders. Lots of remarkable chaps have insignificant shoulders – take, for example, Prime Minister John Major or that famous heart-throb Cary Grant. If the shoulders get you down, head for the Health Club where you can compensate for Mother Nature's 'oversight' by working on certain muscle groups to build bulk where you need it. If you aren't that fussed, all you need is a bit of advice on the art of illusion to look terrific.

You will look uninteresting in a suit that fits too snugly. Since the British cut is the one that follows the shape of a man's figure most closely, this one is not your best. Opt instead for the Modified European cut which will artificially extend your shoulders slightly to help balance your hips and project more strength. The peaked lapels of these suits also create a broadening illusion in the shoulders.

For shirts, unless your neck is short and/or thick, try a cutaway collar which draws the eye out. Your ties need to be significant in width, yet still current with fashion and, of course, balance with the width of your lapels. A narrow tie just emphasises the narrowness of the upper half of your body. Men with thick or short necks need to avoid higher-styled collars. A narrow spread, with longer, pointed tips, creates a welcome vertical 'break', making your neck look less full.

The Apple-Shaped Body

If you have a bit of a paunch, this might be where you belong. This shape can be found among the fit as well as the unfit. Often men who were or are still athletic, with a broad chest, a rounded back and often rounded shoulders – like Frank Bruno – create a round silhouette. Also, portly, overweight men who don't exercise and put on all their weight in their tummy area have the same shape but in their case it is not made of muscle. Some examples would be the late Robert Maxwell, Helmut Kohl and astrologer Russell Grant.

Men of this body type feel most comfortable in the American Sack style suit as well as many trendy European versions of the easy unconstructed look, but these styles do not create a very smart, professional look for work. Instead, the Modified European or the British style are recommended. Often I see such men in huge, overscaled European suits which only make them look larger than life and sometimes quite comical. Go for ease in style, which means single-breasted rather than double-breasted suits. However, really portly men with fluctuating waistlines can cover their girth most effectively in a double-breasted suit, left open. When waistcoats are in style (i.e. three-piece suits) these create an illusion of a narrow spread around the middle and look smart around the office if you want to leave off your jacket sometimes. But bear in mind that you look your least successful when jacketless. So for meetings, even the informal pop into the boss's office, put on your jacket.

In ties, don't choose any that are very boldly patterned. Have fun, by all means, but opt for elegance so that attention isn't drawn down to your tie then possibly to your midriff. For shirts, very crisp cotton poplins can be unforgiving on a full neck which men of this body type often have. Oxford cloths and 'end on end' weaves (in which a coloured thread, such as pink, is mixed with a white thread) are easy to wear and a softer button-down collar is more comfortable.

YOUR PROPORTIONS

A lot of men find that when they go shopping, standard clothes don't fit as well as they should. Either the sleeves of jackets or the length of trousers are always too long or too short. Mr Average could almost be a figment of the manufacturers' imagination – or so you may have come to believe.

Fortunately, men's clothes *are* available in most countries in short, average and long; even extra long for really big men. But you need to select the right lengths in order to create the best balance for your particular body. For example, I have been consulted by men who were average to tall in height but had short legs and arms proportional to the rest of their bodies. If they buy a suit simply according to their height it won't be successful.

Let's look more closely at various Figure 'Faults' or inconsistencies, and see how they can be disguised.

Long Body but Short Legs

If you are short in the legs, the secret is not to swamp yourself in a long jacket. Make sure that the cuts you select end where your bottom does, and your legs will look several inches longer. Very trendy, exaggerated European cut suits (more on those on pages 60–1) are a disaster on you, even if you are average to tall. (Most short men learn to steer clear of them in favour of more classical cuts.) Look for jackets that button high on the waist, not low, almost at the hip. The latter exaggerate the long length on top and make you look even shorter in the leg!

Another tip if you have short legs, is never to wear turn-ups because they create an unnecessary horizontal line which cuts your legs even shorter.

left: European-cut suits make shorter men look shorter, as the eye is drawn down by the larger jacket that buttons low

right: Single-breasted jackets which button higher create an illusion of the wearer being taller and well balanced.

Short Body but Long Legs and Arms

If this description fits you, you may be quite striking in stature, that is, tall, but often fail to realise your potential because you select suits that don't create the balance you require.

Very fitted, neat cuts such as that of the British suit (page 59) are too modest in scale for you, with jackets that aren't long enough to create an illusion of balance. It would be better for you to opt for European style suits that will make your torso appear more significant than it is and reduce the apparent length of your legs. (See photos opposite)

While your shorter friends would be lost in double cuff shirts, for you they are advisable because the extra fabric and detail at the cuff make your arms seem less gangly.

With your great long legs, avoid very close-fitting trousers. Opt rather for ones with some width. Also, turn-ups are a great detail for you and serve to shorten your lengthy expanse.

Wrong

Better

Best

YOUR SCALE

The final element, after considering your basic body shape and proportions, is to be mindful of your scale, that is, your height and bone structure. You might, for instance, be a tall chap but have fine bones; not all tall men are big-boned. Conversely, you could be short but have great strapping bones; you may not necessarily be slight.

Your scale helps to guide you in selecting, fabrics, texture and patterns. If a big chap (height and/or bone structure) wears a tie patterned with small polka dots, it's not so interesting. He needs bold ties (in pattern) to balance with his body.

Men with slight bones or short bodies, or a combination of both, need to steer clear of bold or striking patterns that are very large, opting rather for mid-size or fine designs to create a better balance.

Think about your scale when selecting your accessories. Look at your wrist and the size of your watch. Do you wear it or does it wear you? Are your cufflinks significant enough for a man of your body type, proportions and bone structure?

The key to looking your best is to be mindful of your basics – your shape, proportions and scale. If you weren't dealt an even deck by Mother Nature, try my balancing tips and you will look and feel absolutely perfect!

left: Single-breasted suits, particularly British and American cuts, can make tall men look like beanpoles.

centre: Double-breasted styles are always interesting on tall men who can wear jackets with 6 or 4 buttons. But watch they don't button too high for your proportions, as they do here.

right: The best choice for the long legged is the generous, easy-cut of the Double-breasted European suit. The lower buttoning breaks up your extra length with dash.

CHAPTER 6

CHOOSING A SUIT

GONE are the days when a man went shopping for a suit only to be greeted by a sea of navy or grey in single or double-breasted versions. Today, men are given a wide range of options in terms of colour, weight, texture and cut; in fact, so great is the choice that many men don't quite know where to begin. How often have you gone shopping for clothes, determined to buy something different this time, only to return with much the same as before because you weren't at all confident that the new looks were for you, even if you found the courage to try them on.

That, of course, was before you understood your colouring, body shape and proportions and had seriously thought about the image you want and need to project in your present position. Now, you will-find that choosing a suit becomes much easier. But first let's consider the different types of suits available today. What you'll find in the shops and department stores will be variations of one or more of these four basic styles:

British/Savile Row

European Cut

Modified European Cut

American Sack

THE BRITISH/SAVILE ROW SUIT

The British Suit is renowned for its tailored 'drape' as it was originally known in the 1930s. Men who don't study fashion trends like this style of suit because it feels more tailored and stays with them when they move around; like armour, their European detractors might add! Savile Row tailors proudly explain that the men prefer a cut that follows the natural line of their body rather than styles that try to transform the body with exaggerated shoulders and narrow hips.

Single-breasted British/Savile Row jacket with double vents at back

and simple notched lapels

The shoulders are slightly padded but never artificially extended, as with the European cut suit. The waist is defined and nipped-in, and accentuated by double vents at the back. Double-vents are especially flattering on larger-bottomed men who feel too constrained in ventless European suits.

The pockets are flapped and slightly angled. The most traditional will have a third pocket for loose change but this is usually a special feature of bespoke tailoring. Most off-the-peg British suits have two outside pockets (not including the breast pocket).

The single-breasted suit has simple notched lapels (as shown) which are more modest in scale than those on European single-breasted suits.

The British double-breasted suit boasts the same tailored construction as the single-breasted models and is available with four or six buttons (never just two like many European designs).

In America, this style of suit is referred to as the Updated American cut, which often has the centre vent so preferred by American men. But this suit's origins remain that of Britain's Savile Row.

The European suit can be double- or single-breasted. Both versions are ventless

THE EUROPEAN CUT SUIT

Here's the suit for which the 1980s will be remembered. Traditional tailoring went out of the window when mainly German and Italian designers decided to remake the suit. Layers of construction inside the suit were abandoned in favour of minimalist tailoring to give men a new ease of movement. Shoulders were widened, in 1930s style, jackets lengthened and trousers were given more ease and volume. The look could be sharp or relaxed, depending upon the wearer's attitude, as well as the suit's colour and cloth.

The double-breasted Euro suit comes with two or six buttons, generally. All button quite low, creating an illusion of the top half being longer than the bottom half. Hence, this is a dangerous style for men under 6ft (1.8m) tall. The jackets can end three inches (7.5cm) below the curve of the buttocks, which can make even the lankiest man look squat.

The worst excess of the severely padded shoulders has waned in favour of a more natural shoulder line, but this type of suit is still more exaggerated at the shoulders than other cuts. The new ease has evolved along with the new popularity of the single-breasted versions, winning favour with a generation of men who have only ever owned double-breasted suits.

The lapels of the European suit are wider than other cuts, hence they always require a bold tie in both width and pattern.

The European suit emphasises the shoulders and the hips without taking too much notice of the waist (unlike the British and Modified Euro cuts). Jackets are ventless, which requires most men to unbutton immediately upon, if not before, sitting down. A ventless suit is best on men with flat bottoms.

Despite its availability in shorter fittings, this cut does little to enhance the stature of the short man, who is better served by the stylish Modified versions of the European suit.

THE MODIFIED EUROPEAN-CUT SUIT

The six-button, double-breasted, modified European-Cut suit buttons in the middle and has simple notched lapels

This traditional continental suit is more fitted than today's European suits but not so fitted as the British suit. It was most popular before the mid 1980s, when many Italian, German and a few French designers decided to deconstruct their suits in favour of more comfort.

Today, mainly the French, but also Italian and British companies, produce beautiful examples of this suit. I describe it as the Modified European-cut because it looks more polished and fitted than the looser, often overscaled, European suit.

Here is the suit for the man who wants a bit more flair than the traditional British or Updated American suit but who can't abide the often shapeless silhouettes of today's European suits, popular though they may be at both designer and discount prices. The armholes are high so they neatly 'hug' across the chest. The six button double-breasted version generally buttons in the middle, with the bottom one left undone to emphasise the waist. This silhouette is very flattering on many men, especially those of short to average height.

The single-breasted versions sometimes have a centre vent (the French like these), with simple notched lapels more in scale with the British rather than the European cut. The pockets are often slashed, which is most flattering on men with ample hips (flap pockets create bulk and attention where you don't need or want it). The trousers have minimal volume, which can make sitting down and crossing your legs American-style, that is, with your foot crossed over your opposite knee and leg open wide, tricky.

The Modified European-cut suit is best on men who aspire to an elegant look. The neatness of the cut means it's not a recommended option for rough, tough natural guys who need the more generous room of the European suit or the protective armour of the British cut.

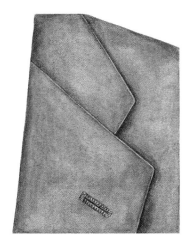

The American Sack has notched and rolled lapels and pocket flaps

THE AMERICAN SACK

Also known in America as the 'natural shoulder' cut suit as it was developed with no padding to define the shoulders. The look is square and boxy and it is much shorter in length than European designs. The modest-width lapels are notched but 'rolled', giving them a softer, less defined edge than other cuts. The pockets always have flaps. And the rear always sports a centre vent.

The only style variations in the Sack come with the occasional switch from two to three buttons and from a slight nip at the waist.

Don't think this suit is found only on continental USA. The Sack might have originated around the turn of the century in America, but today some European manufacturers produce their own interpretations of this easy-to-wear, relaxed suit. The Sack's ample shape means that men with square or full bodies often enjoy its comfort over other cuts. If their waistlines are fuller than their chest or even their shoulders, then the good old Sack will accommodate them more easily than any other model. But it is nearly impossible to look smart or sharp in the Sack, so it is not advisable to wear it for business, although too many American men have yet to appreciate this fact.

FASHION FORWARD LOOKS

Unless you work for the likes of Jean Paul Gaultier or Yohji Yamamoto, present a Style Programme on TV, promote high fashion, or simply have lots of spare cash to spend on trendy threads for after work, suits in extreme styles have no place in your wardrobe – certainly not your business wardrobe. Female colleagues may appreciate the flair and individuality of a new look, but any fashion statement tried out on male colleagues, superiors and customers will be completely lost if you work outside the fashion world. Also, you are likely to be perceived as rebellious and challenging everything the organisation stands for. So, it's not recommended that you invest in bizarre styles, extreme fabrics or colours, no matter how wonderful they might be, when you are buying for your business wardrobe.

Today, many young men in business like to push the limits of the corporate culture by adopting an image that's more creative and individual. Extremely talented, rising stars have been sent to me for 'sorting out' after wearing 'green suits' in the financial services sector, or for sporting ear-rings in computer sales and adopting hair extensions, i.e. ponytails, when marketing petrochemicals. Employers today may find it more difficult to fire people outright, simply for adopting a contrary or bad appearance, but increasingly they are seeking the help of image consultants to convince these dissentients that they are shooting themselves in the career foot by affronting the corporate image. Many young men do want to be more expressive with their own style and feel frustrated wearing the neutral, to them bland, corporate 'uniforms' which I describe in this book as classic and appropriate for most business situations.

But it is possible to look interesting and individual without offending colleagues and ruining your career prospects. Instead of a really bizarre (not to you but to the real world of average business people), overscale or extremely cut suit, opt for a fashionable European cut in a fabric and colour that's subtly different from those worn by most of your colleagues. If you're surrounded by pin-stripes or solids, try a fine weave with interesting flecks of colour that are only discernible close up. Now team it with a white shirt with a hint of another colour – not the one that shouts 'here comes the pink shirt' – but has just a slight pink cast. Select your ties from quality shops but choose untraditional patterns. Resist a tendency to choose patterns that scream; if the pattern *is* strange, keep it medium to small in scale. The effect will be an interesting image that's unique but not offensive. The details won't overwhelm but will make an individual and memorable statement.

BUYING A SUIT: RECOGNISING QUALITY

Too many men adopt the attitude that a suit is a suit is a suit. Nothing could be further from the truth. What distinguishes suits is not their prices necessarily, although good quality in suits doesn't come cheaply, nor is it their labels. It is their details that make a statement. Some of these distinguishing details are obvious, like the stripes meticulously matching up at the pockets or the seams or good quality fabric but others – the most important details – are invisible to the undiscerning eye, that is, they are part of the construction of the suit.

A good suit is partially hand-made. No machine can duplicate hand-tailoring when it comes to making a suit look and feel its best on a man. That is not to say that tedious jobs like cutting, doing buttonholes, and hems are not better done by machines. But when it comes to sewing on suit collars, constructing the interfacing and attaching the sleeves to the shoulders, no machine can do the job with the skill of a tailor.

To see how your suits measure up, turn over the collars and inspect the stitching underneath. If it is perfectly straight and even, it has been done on a flat surface by a machine. If it looks like something your mother might have sewn, slightly irregular with each stitch of minutely differing size, then it has been hand-sewn by a tailor, over his lap. The fact that it is sewn over a curved surface, actually the tailor's thigh, means that the collar will hug your neck better (because your neck is also round). If yours were machine-stitched, this is almost certainly why some or all of your collars stick out away from your neck, which is particularly noticeable when you are seated. Watch news readers on television and see if you can see who has the better suits. (BBC's Martin Lewis is tops in Britain.)

Now, with the jacket on, feel the fabric over your chest. Is the fabric smooth or does it feel hard and stiff? Take the jacket off and see if you can separate the lining from the suiting fabric. If you can't, then the two materials have been fused with glue, again by machine, which is a faster and cheaper process used by many manufacturers (you would be surprised by the number of 'designer labels' that reveal this shortcut!). If a lining *is* fused, it won't last very long. Eventually, it will feel very puckered inside the jacket – especially after about the third dry-cleaning – and no amount of pressing will rectify the fault, indeed, it may make matters worse. So – avoid suits with fused linings.

Check that the pattern of the suit, if it has one, lines up at the seams and pockets (see opposite). This is particularly important for pin-stripes which look awful when not matched. You'll often find this mis-match on less expensive suits because the manufacturer has kept costs down by not 'wasting' fabric in order to match up perfectly. Seams, too, may be less generous on cheaper suits and they can have an uncomfortably 'snug' fit.

The armholes should be comfortable and, again, will feel much better if hand-sewn. Ask your sales assistant if the suit you are considering has hand-work here as it can be difficult to tell without taking the jacket apart.

Selecting Fabrics

You will have endless choice in colour, weaves, texture and weight but you have none when it comes to choosing man-made rather than natural fibres. You can see a polyester suit across the room. Men who wear them gener-

Quality patterned suits match up at critical points like pocket seams

Man-handle a fabric to get a real feel for the cloth

ally hate their suits, finding them uncomfortable, and shedding them as soon as they leave the office. Man-made fibres simply don't breathe so heat gets trapped inside, making you feel as if you are in a sauna whenever the sun comes out.

Wool, in its many weights and qualities is the recommended fabric for suits. Even in the summertime a cool or lightweight wool is preferable to cotton, linen or silk blends, unless you work in a very, very warm climate. Wool breathes, keeps its shape and is more durable than other natural fibres.

The finer the feel of the fabric, the better the quality. To test it, scrunch up the fabric in your hand (see above). How does it feel? Is it scratchy and rough, or smooth to the touch? How well does it respond to your scrunch? Does it wrinkle easily? Do the wrinkles remain when you release your hold, or do they fall out quickly?

When your suits are made of a natural fibre like wool, you do, however, need to rest them between wearings to allow the fibres to spring back into shape. Also, don't overstress the cloth with excessive dry-cleaning, a process which involves the use of harsh chemicals that reduce the life of a suit. Better to hang the suits to air outside or outside the wardrobe, and then store in the wardrobe on the wooden hangers specifically designed for suits.

Taking care of good quality suits means a suit press is your most valuable home appliance. You can press your trousers so they always look fresh and then hang them and the matching jacket to rest for at least 24 hours before storing in your wardrobe. Ensure that each suit is allowed sufficient space, too; if your wardrobe is crowded, check whether some items can be stored in cupboards or chests to make more room.

Suiting weights   Understand about the various weight of suiting fabrics and you will be able to ensure you get what you need to be comfortable in your regular working environment, or to wear when travelling to different climates. Nothing gives away the foreigner abroad more than if he comes from a warm climate wearing an inappropriate lightweight suit (and often light colour as well) to a cold country in the northern hemisphere; or if he comes from a very temperate climate and wears a dark, heavyweight suit in a hot environment.

Traditionally, suits were measured by their weight in ounces per yard, but many today have gone metric and are measured in grams per metre. Here's a guide of what to look for to suit different climates and seasons.

Standard Weight	Metric Equivalent	Description
5–6 oz	185–200 grams	Tropical weight/almost paperweight
8–9 oz	250 grams	Lightweight suiting for warm summers and climates
11–13 oz	350–400 grams	Medium, winterweight suiting
14–15 oz	450–500 grams	Heavy, outdoor jackets & suiting

Double or Single Breasted?

Fashion has a lot to do with your suits looking current or dated. Fortunately, men's fashion changes at a snail's pace compared to women's!

For the last five years or so, the double-breasted suit has reigned supreme. But the suit needed to be either two button – those very sleek Italian numbers – or six button – the real 'high-powered' 1980s suit. The four button double-breasted suit is more classic and remains the safest option for the most conservative men.

The 1990s welcome the return of the single-breasted suit which is preferred by many men for its ease in buttoning and unbuttoning. Single-breasted suits are also better in the spring and summertime, when you can do without the added panel of wool insulation you get with a double-breasted suit. To ensure that your new single-breasted suit looks current, not a 10-year-old version, select one that buttons high (three buttons) or low (one button). The two button single-breasted suit is the most classic.

Two or Three Pieces

The three-piece suit, once the purview of the most traditional, 'buttoned-up' man, is now selected by the trendiest with new look three-piece suits offered by many designers in all cuts, that is, American, European (fashion-forward and modified cuts) and British. The waistcoat is flattering on the thin and thick-set alike. It adds bulk for the leanest and covers the girth of the portly more effectively than a single-breasted jacket on its own.

Wearing a waistcoat without a jacket around the office allows a more polished image than just going around in a shirt alone. So, do consider a three-piece suit for an elegant look as well as for its variety; you can wear the suit with or without the waistcoat, and the waistcoat with or without the jacket.

PROPER FIT

No matter how wonderful the fabric or impressive the label, a suit that doesn't fit properly will look half the price you paid for it and not be enjoyable to wear. After years of shopping with men I know all the tricks of self-deception that go on in front of a three-way mirror, so here are some tips to guide you in assessing whether or not a suit actually fits you.

Size

Depending on the cut of suit, size can vary, sometimes considerably. So if you think you are a 42 Regular but try on a European cut suit and it swamps you, don't panic and think that you've got some wasting disease. European cuts are far more generous than others so it's really a case of trial and error to find a good fit, particularly in the lower price categories.

If it has been a while since you have bought a good quality suit get yourself re-measured by one of the trained sales assistants in a good men's store. If the idea of getting measured sounds embarrassing, here's a guide to doing it at home – though you will still need help because some measurements are impossible to take yourself, such as inside leg and sleeve lengths.

How to Take Your Measurements

Take a tape measure, new enough not to have stretched – making your measurements inaccurate – and follow these guidelines.

Measure yourself when wearing only your pants and don't pull the tape too tightly. There's no point in cheating to get a smaller measurement as you'll only be uncomfortable in your clothes.

Where to measure

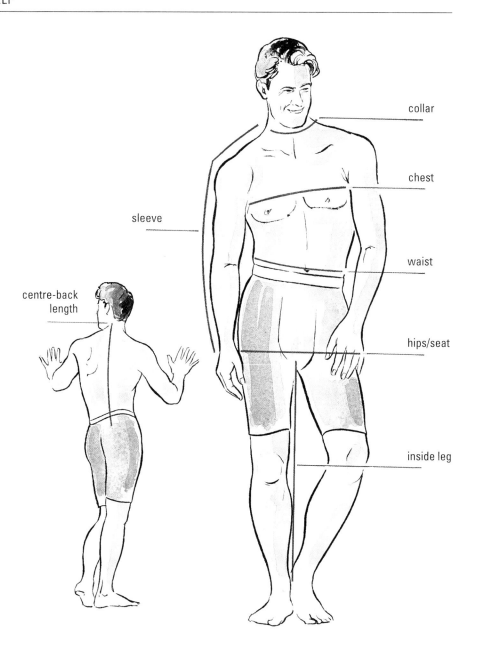

collar

chest

sleeve

waist

centre-back
length

hips/seat

inside leg

- **Collar**: measure around the base of the neck.

- **Chest**: measure under the arm-pits. Make sure the tape is on a straight horizontal line all round your chest and going across the middle of your shoulder-blade, not under it.

- **Waist**: measure round the natural waistline. Try the top of your boxer shorts. With Y-fronts, face the mirror and find your natural waist. It should be distinguishable.

- **Hips/Seat**: measure around the broadest part of your beam, ensuring that the tape is kept on an even horizontal line.

- **Sleeve**: measure from the base of your neck, straight along the shoulder-line and down over the elbow to the wristbone.

- **Inside leg**: measure from the top of the inside leg to the ankle bone.

- **Centre-back length**: This measurement varies with the cut of the suit.

READY TO WEAR, OFF THE PEG SIZES

- Suit and jacket sizes range from 34 to 44 inches and trouser sizes range from 28 to 38 inches

- Standard suit sizes allow for 6 inches difference between chest and waist e.g. 34 inch chest, 28 inch waist; 40 inch chest, 34 inch waist.

- Suit sizes conform to size of chest.

Measuring for Suits and Jackets (UK and USA)

Jacket	Your size is:						
	34	**36**	**38**	**40**	**42**	**44**	**46**
	If you measure (in inches):						
Chest	34	36	38	40	42	44	46
Sleeve	31	$31\frac{1}{2}$	32	$32\frac{1}{2}$	33	$33\frac{1}{2}$	34
Waist	28	30	32	34	36	38	40
Seat/Bottom	35	37	39	41	43	45	47
Length (regular)	29	$29\frac{1}{2}$	30	$30\frac{1}{2}$	31	$31\frac{1}{2}$	32

Trousers	Your size is:						
	28	**30**	**32**	**34**	**36**	**38**	**40**
	If you measure (in inches):						
Waist	28	30	32	34	36	38	40
Seat/Bottom	35	37	39	41	43	45	47

Measuring for Suits and Jackets (Europe)

Jacket Your size is:

	44	46	48	50	52	54	56
	If you measure (in cms):						
Chest	81	92	97	102	107	112	117
Sleeve	79	80	81	82	84	85	86
Waist	71	76	82	87	92	97	102
Seat/Bottom	89	94	99	104	109	115	120
Length (regular)	74	75	77	78	79	80	81

Trousers Your size is:

	71	76	82	87	92	97	102
	If you measure (in cms):						
Waist	71	76	82	87	92	97	102
Seat/Bottom	71	94	99	105	97	115	120

International Sizing Guides

Suits, jackets, sweaters, sportswear

UK/USA	36	38	40	42	44	46	48
Europe	46	48	50	52	54	56	58

Shirts

UK/US	14	$14\frac{1}{2}$	15	$15\frac{1}{2}$	16	$16\frac{1}{2}$	17	$17\frac{1}{2}$	18
Europe	36	37	38	39	40	41	42	43	44

Shoes

UK	$5\frac{1}{2}$	6	$6\frac{1}{2}$	7	$7\frac{1}{2}$	8	$8\frac{1}{2}$	9	$9\frac{1}{2}$	10	
Europe	$39\frac{1}{2}$	40	$40\frac{1}{2}$	41	$41\frac{1}{2}$	42	$42\frac{1}{2}$	43	$43\frac{1}{2}$	44	
US	$5\frac{1}{2}$	$6\frac{1}{2}$	7	$7\frac{1}{2}$	8	$8\frac{1}{2}$	9	$9\frac{1}{2}$	10	$10\frac{1}{2}$	

YOUR SUIT: GETTING THE FIT RIGHT

When shopping for a new suit, be sure you are wearing a business shirt, tie, belt and your weekday shoes. If shopping on a Saturday in jeans, a T-shirt and trainers you won't be able to tell if the suit fits or not. That is why I always advise men to shop during the week when they are dressed in their normal business clothes. Besides the shops being less crowded during the week, you are more likely to be attended by someone who is knowledgeable and skilled. Many shops now employ relief staff for Saturday work and, however well meaning, they are not usually as experienced.

The Jacket

If the jacket does not work, it isn't even worth trying on the trousers. So try the jacket on first. Always try garments on in front of a full-length mirror, preferably with at least a second one angled so that you can see the back view without contorting your body. Three-way mirrors are best of all. Button up the jacket. From the front, do the lapels sit smoothly against your chest or do they stick out? If the latter is the case, the jacket is too tight.

Notice where and how the jacket buttons; is there any pulling? Often a minor adjustment is all that's required to correct this. Does it gape at the buttons? This often relates to a 'drop shoulder', usually the right shoulder on men, due to years of carrying a heavy attaché or briefcase. This is where a good fitter can make all the difference. But there will be a limit on the amount of adjusting a jacket can take before it begins to look like a patchwork. Beware of any fitter who cavalierly dismisses any and all problems as surmountable. You don't want a jacket that needs so many nips and tucks that it loses its shape nor do you want the bill that usually accompanies such alterations. Take your custom elsewhere.

Everything should line up – the lapels should balance, the shoulders should be even (especially if yours aren't). A little extra padding on one shoulder is easy) and the collar should fit snugly around your neck and not gape. Check also that you can bend your arms comfortably.

Take a look in the mirror to see how the back fits. Do you notice any pulling across the shoulders? British and Modified European cut suits will feel more fitted than the looser European ones but they should not feel tight. Stretch your arms out straight, reach up. Is the suit straining? When buttoned-up, can you see horizontal 'pull-marks' across the back? If so, the jacket is too tight. If, conversely, you notice vertical folds, then the jacket is probably too big. (See page 72) However, remember that European cut suits will be more generous across the shoulders and back.

Now check the fit across the bottom. If the jacket is double-vented, the

Check how the back fits by looking in a mirror. Do you see any horizontal or vertical lines?

too tight

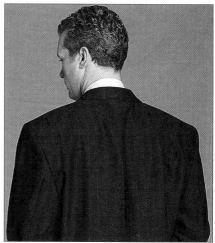

too big

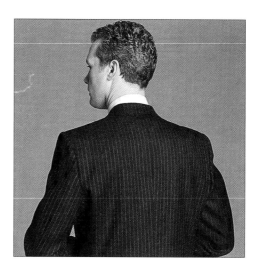

proper fit

vents should be closed when the jacket is buttoned and you are standing. If they are open, the suit is too tight for you; try the next size up.

Ventless suits (i.e. European cut) should fit easily across the bottom allowing for freedom of movement. If your hips are ample this cut can be unforgiving. Try double vents instead.

Move around. Put the jacket on and take it off. Bend, reach-up, sit down, cross your legs. Get the feel of the jacket. If single-breasted, make sure it is comfortable when buttoned. If double-breasted and worn undone do you look lost inside it? Double-breasted suits, especially the European cut, can overwhelm a man with a slight build no matter what his height. And although the double-breasted jacket is intended to be buttoned when not seated, many men wear them open when in the office, so they need to look good with the jacket open as well as when buttoned.

Trousers

If the jacket fits, then it's worth trying on the trousers. Like most men, you probably have definite ideas about what you need in trousers in terms of fit. Some are preoccupied with having ample space for their private parts. However, insisting on trousers with a crotch that extends to mid-thigh is, and looks, ridiculous. Be assured that the sales assistant will be aware of this important consideration and you will be asked on which side you 'prefer to dress yourself', that is, right or left trouser leg. Once that's determined, the fitter can make extra adjustments for comfort. Sit down, cross your legs, do a knee bend to determine if you have the best fit possible.

Finding your waistline   And what about the waistline? How does that feel? Your waist is that midline point below the ribs, above the hips about smack-dab on your navel. It is *not* below the tummy, a few millimetres above the hips. The secret of a comfortable fit is to get the 'rise of the trousers' – i.e. the distance between the crotch and the waist – to come as close to matching your own as possible.

Wearing your belt you want the waist of your trousers to be snug but not overly so – allow for the occasional three-course lunch to be enjoyed in comfort. If your waistline is your most fluctuating measurement, consider getting trousers with braces which allow more freedom and movement. However, if intending to wear braces in lieu of a belt, never buy trousers with a tight fit as you could damage yourself when you sit down!

Length   Buying trousers off the peg with turn-ups or hems already finished is a risky business. Length is very individual and rarely catered for with standard manufacturing. Whether to have turn-ups or not depends on your legs. As I mentioned earlier, when discussing proportions, if short-legged, it is best to avoid turn-ups no matter how stylish they might be. That extra, albeit slight, horizontal line visually chops another couple of inches off your legs. Conversely, turn-ups are recommended for men with long legs.

The trouser hemline, uncuffed, should never be even all the way round, i.e. the same length in the front and back. Aim for a lower drop of about one and a half inches in the back. On the front of the shoe, the trousers should just 'break', i.e. more than reach the shoe and hit it folding slightly inwards so we don't see the top 2–3 shoelaces.

As with your jacket, check the trouser fit across the hips and bottom. A good tailor can tighten or ease trouser seams within limits – the better the suit the more fabric to play with. Make sure the pockets lie flat even when you have added some change and keys. If the pockets are stitched, ask for them to be snipped open for you to see the effect.

TAKE YOUR POCKETS IN HAND

It's time to break some bad habits: too many men load their pockets so full that no matter how terrifically a suit fits or how expensive it is, it will look like rubbish. Here are the caveats on what to carry where:

Inside Breast Pocket

- a slim diary

- envelope style wallet with credit cards and notes

- a slim note pad and/or calculator

- a pen set

Outside Breast Pocket

- a silk pocket handkerchief only!

Outside Front Pockets

- business card holder

- nothing else aside from the odd notes/messages passed on throughout the day (empty each evening)

Side Trouser Pockets

- loose change

- a few, essential keys

Back Trouser Pockets

- a slim wallet (in lieu of carrying it in the breast pocket) but only if you are blessed with a flat bottom.

COATS: OVER, TRENCH OR RAIN

All men working in a temperate climate or travelling to the northern hemisphere on business need at least one overcoat and a 'mac', that is, a rain or trenchcoat, to protect themselves and their suits from the wet and the cold.

Overcoats are usually made of wool and are most practical in a dark, neutral colour such as navy, olive, burgundy, charcoal or black. Avoid trendy 'fashion-forward' styles which may put off your more traditional business associates and also date too quickly, making your investment in an overcoat short-term. As an overcoat costs two to three times that of a suit, it is a serious investment. If well-chosen it can, and should, last five years or more.

Select a classic style and one that is comfortable enough to wear with a suit underneath. To make sure, shop for one when you are wearing a suit.

- Shorter men are better in simple, single-breasted styles, such as the Chesterfield or Greatcoat. Belted styles or double-breasted coats such as the British Warm only serve to 'chop you in half' and look wider. The length is best if just below the knee.

- Tall men should avoid snug-fitting, single-breasted coats and ones that are very long; they just make you look like a beanpole! Try double-breasted and belted models that are no longer than mid-calf.

Rain or Trench Coats are more versatile and less expensive than overcoats, hence they are becoming increasingly popular as the first or only coat investment in many men's wardrobes. If you don't like the formal finish of an overcoat in winter, the year-round mackintosh with removable linings might be your best bet. Be careful when choosing the fabric: it should be neither too dark (so dreary in the spring), nor too light (which shows the dirt too quickly). Most macs are not waterproof but merely water-resistant, and they need repeated spraying with 'Scotch Guard' after dry cleaning, if they are to keep you dry in a downpour.

If you want just one coat, and opt for a mac, appreciate that you'll need to replace it *bi-annually* if you wear it for 25 weeks or more a year. Don't degenerate into an 'Inspector Colombo', looking as if you have just rolled out from underneath a rock in your mac when you make your all important entrance to meetings with colleagues or clients. Your coat needs to indicate what's to be expected underneath, so be sure yours doesn't let your image down.

CHAPTER 7

A WORKING WARDROBE

TAKE a good look at your current collection of suits, shirts and ties. How many of your suits are in good condition, fit, and are not dated? Don't include any that are marginal – you know, the favourite relics that have given you lots of wear or any that are merely passable. To protect a successful image you need clothes that are in top condition, and of the best quality you can afford. You know this after reading the preceding sections on colour, body shape, proportions, scale and height, so be ruthless about the suits that fall way short of being flattering on you.

A wardrobe requires versatility if it is going to work *for* you, not *against* you. Be sure that it can live up to the demands of your position. Are there suits, shirts and ties ready for your next presentation, client meeting, dinner with senior management, weekend business conference? Do you ask a lot of the few suits you have, expecting them to create a positive impression regardless of the circumstance?

Many of my clients have plentiful wardrobes but, even so, their clothes are 'much of a muchness', without the variety that would indicate they know how to make subtle adjustments to suit different occasions. Other men I have worked with are so keen on men's fashion that their suits and ties are *too* memorable so that whatever they wear, the reaction will be: 'Oh, he's wearing that again.'

To get the most benefit from your clothing investments, start with the **basics**. These are the quality, versatile components that you can continually 're-create' and make look new, fresh and interesting over and over. You might think *boring* when you see the list of suggested suits for your working wardrobe – but what I recommend will work for most men, of any age, in most businesses or professions, in most countries.

Having read Chapter Two *The Industry, The Image*, it's up to you to decide how to adapt the advice given therein. If you need to be more conservative or should be a little more adventurous because of the Company's image and client/customer expectations then follow your instinct. If you work in a country like The Netherlands, Australia and New Zealand, or a region like Scandinavia or the southern states of America where the business culture is a 'suitless' one, you will only need one suit for formal occasions and can have great fun selecting sports jackets, blazers and trousers to develop your successful image wardrobe. The only caveat is to remember if and when you ever travel on business, to play it safe and buy another appropriate suit to impress people with your international savoir faire.

SEVEN BASIC WARDROBE COMPONENTS

The Navy Suit

For projecting authority nothing works better than a navy blue suit. Remember the guidelines about your own personal colouring when selecting yours, that is, whether it should be a dark or light version. When this is teamed with your white (pure, ivory or soft white) you will have the most serious business look (think of the policeman's uniform).

Choose the style with care, following the guidelines given for your body shape in Chapter Five.

If you really want to impress, choose a double-breasted navy suit – which is even more formal than the single-breasted suit. If beautifully cut, of good quality and a medium weight, this suit can be worn year round and will always help you to be taken seriously. If you are below average height, look for a six-button model which buttons in the middle; don't choose a four-button style.

The value of the traditional navy business suit is that it is not memorable and can be worn a couple of times a week without people realising it, provided you are creative with your shirt, tie and (occasional) pocket handkerchief combinations. If wearing a white shirt, always enliven the look with a patterned tie and plain or patterned, though not matching, pocket handkerchief. If everything is plain the look will be severe and uninspired. Boldly striped shirts were designed to be framed by navy, making both the suit and shirt look wonderful.

So, if your wardrobe doesn't contain a navy suit or the one you have has seen better days put it down on your Shopping List as your first investment priority.

left to right: The Navy Suit, the Grey Suit, the Coloured Suit

The Grey Suit

Here we have the second traditional business colour which is equally as versatile as navy. Grey, even in the deepest charcoal, is more approachable and 'user-friendly' than navy, so it is warmly recommended for those days when you really need to get people to open up. If you have Warm colouring, choose a grey with brown in it rather than with a blue undertone (the latter is great on Cool types). Don't be boring and wear just white shirts with this suit; grey comes alive when teamed with a pastel or icy colour like the palest blue, pink, lilac or peach.

Light grey suits, no matter how expensive, seldom reflect their cost, whereas you can get away with a more moderately priced charcoal because it will always look top of the line provided the cut of the suit flatters you.

The Coloured Suit

Depending on your job and the organisation within which you work, increasingly there are opportunities for men to wear *new neutrals* such as olive, aubergine, pewter, teal, slate or jade. In many businesses these make a welcome change from the smart but conventional navies and greys and can look equally professional and polished if worn correctly.

The key to success in wearing these less traditional colours is to buy good quality and to ensure the fit is first rate. Also, if you are uncertain about the acceptability of a new colour, play it safer in your shirts and ties. Be cautious about wearing these less traditional colours in new situations, such as when meeting new clients or travelling abroad. On such occasions, it is safest to wear the more internationally acceptable navies and greys.

The Pin-Stripe Suit

Let me first anticipate and deal with the outcries from younger and European readers who think that because I am based in Britain I naturally have a penchant for pin-stripes which might be considered quintessentially English. From my work with top companies in North America, the EEC and in the Far East I can assure you that a selectively chosen pin-stripe looks elegant anywhere. However, do not sport the traditional chalk stripe. This, I think, has had its day and does look out of place anywhere but in the United Kingdom.

Today there are endless versions of the pin-stripe, both in weave and in colour. If you are considering an investment in a pin-stripe, go for one with a coloured stripe (or even two colours) that are only discernible upon close inspection. When you buy it, also select two or three ties incorporating the colours of the stripes.

When attempting to mix patterns in shirts and ties with your pin-stripes beware that a striped shirt with such a suit creates a dizzying effect. Studies have shown that people who have to work with men who wear boldly striped suits and shirts are more prone to migraines than workers with more subtly attired colleagues. You can wear a striped tie with a pin-stripe suit but make sure that the width of the stripes vary in size. Better still, try a pattern or bold abstract which will offset the pin-stripes with more dash.

The Prince of Wales Check

Just the mention of *checks* makes some men weak. For checks to succeed in business or professional life they must be subtle; don't choose a suit that can be spotted among a crowd or from a block away. Also only select checks if you are average to tall in height and of average build.

The Prince of Wales is a beautiful weave that is made up in countless variations. For those 'business/social' events, such as a day out at the races, here's the suit that is appropriately stylish. For less sober industries like advertising, training, management consulting and retailing it also makes a welcome alternative to the traditional business suit.

Other checks, in subtle colours that are recommended in your colour palette, would be an option as suit number four in your wardrobe. If you work

left to right: The Pinstripe Suit, the Prince of Wales Check Suit

in a warm, sunny climate this can be more medium, even light in tone (if recommended for your colouring).

Mixing patterns in your shirts and ties when these are worn with a check suit requires thought. The best shirt choice will be your white one or a very pale pastel. A white with a soft grey stripe is also fun with the Prince of Wales check. When selecting your tie, always go for a pattern with some red in it, as that colour offsets this weave more beautifully than any other. The ties that look a bit strange are florals and strong abstracts. The Prince of Wales is elegant, timeless and traditional. Do it justice with a classic (not boring) foulard or medium-scale polka dot. A solid red pocket handkerchief is the finishing touch highly recommended.

The Blazer/Sports-jacket

By the turn of the century, many men will go to the office in more relaxed clothes than they do today. In America, many companies now have 'casual days', when staff are allowed to wear whatever they like. In warmer climates, fussy, formal suits, even if lightweight, are impractical. In Singapore and many Far Eastern countries, business shirts and trousers are the norm. The more liberties you take in dressing down at the office the greater the risk you run in jeopardising your image, especially if you work in traditional sectors or for conservative management.

But all successful men know that they need a smart 'dressed-down' look for those more relaxed social occasions and those that take place away from the office. Also, this is an acceptable way to dress in many cultures and in certain organisations. With more entrepreneurs and home-based operations, a smart jacket and trousers may be all that's needed for most meetings, except the heavy-duty ones, say, with one's board or bankers (both of which require a suit).

When in doubt, a navy blazer with grey, burgundy, taupe, stone, or denim trousers cuts a dashing image for relaxed social occasions with professional or business colleagues. It is also recommended for those weekend seminars or conferences when everyone is told to dress 'casually' and men turn up in everything from their usual workaday business suit to tracksuits and sneakers. These occasions call for a less formal but still a 'quasi-business' dress to create a smart, noteworthy image among the unimaginatively suited drones and the out-of-place tracksuited sporting types.

If you take your image seriously, and want to create a good impression with friends as well as business associates, your wardrobe will require a blazer or tweed sports-jacket for the winter and for a summer version in linen, washed silk or seersucker. This is where you must have more fun with your colour palette and explore possibilities beyond navy and grey. Plain or solid colours are safest but try a subtle pattern for variety and understated flair. Just don't go too wild in mixing patterns until you are confident that it works. Try two patterns to start, perhaps teaming a tweedy jacket and a paisley tie or a herringbone jacket with a tattersall shirt. Keep everything else related in colour but plain.

The most elegant look in smart casual wear is to keep the bottom half (i.e. below the belt) simple. Avoid patterned trousers. (Americans and Dutchmen please take note!). Have all the action, excitement in colours, patterns and fabrics near your face, that is, in your jacket, shirt and tie.

Beware of mixing extreme styles that never belong together, such as a silk shirt with your tweed jacket; corduroy trousers and a linen jacket; or a woollen tie with your slick, city jacket. Aim for a harmonious balance in both fabrics and colours, and you've got it!

The Dinner Jacket

The higher you rise and the more city-centred your life, sooner or later the dinner jacket (or DJ) becomes a serious wardrobe consideration. If you are required to wear one more than twice a year, and your weight and suit size stays relatively constant, a well-tailored DJ of superb cut and classic style will be an investment to last you years. The ill-fitted 'penguins' in their last-minute hired tuxedo can be spotted at every formal event. As you climb the

left to right: The Sports
Jacket, the Dinner
Jacket

success ladder and use dinner-dances, charity events and other formal occasions as opportunities to network with your peers, you'll want to be sure that your DJ does you justice. If your colouring is light, warm or soft, the sharp contrast of black and white can be overpowering. Soften the impact of the black and white with more flattering colours in your waistcoat and tie. Increasingly you can find other alternatives but, remember, coloured tuxedos and pastel shirts look provincial, never urbane.

On occasions when everyone else is dressed in much the same uniform, you need to stand out and be noticed. To project individuality, wear a patterned waistcoat or an interesting bow tie and colourful pocket handkerchief.

SHIRTS OF DISTINCTION

Many of the men I have worked with have had little appreciation of the different qualities and fabrics now used in men's business shirts. Gone are the days when your choice was limited to blue or white with a few stripes thrown in for variety. Today you are bombarded with choices in colour, fabric and styling. But the greater the choice the more room for getting it wrong.

Fabric

Let's consider fabric first. The viable options are quite simple: 100 per cent cotton or a cotton-blend that is predominantly cotton (that is, 60 per cent or more). The former is recommended for regular business wear and the latter, the blends which resist creases better, are easier when travelling (unless you happen to be a most fastidious packer).

Cotton comes in many qualities. On the high street, you can find 100 per cent cotton shirts at very good prices, but if you don't know how to distinguish the qualities of cotton you could end up with one of those shirts that is a nightmare to iron. The ideal cotton for your business shirts is poplin which is a plain weave and provides almost a subtle sheen, looking crisp and smart with any business suit. Even better, for their superior quality, feel and price, are the Sea-Island and Egyptian cottons. Shop around; and ask sales assistants if any of their brands are especially easy to iron. They should have this product information.

Softer cotton weaves like the Oxford cloth or end-on-end are more relaxed fabrics, so the collars aren't as stiff. Unfortunately these shirts conflict in style and texture with a formal business suit, although widely seen in the last few years on a lot of younger men. These less formal cottons are more acceptable in smaller companies with a more flexible image and friendly ambience. Men working outside large city centres who opt for smart sports jackets or blazers at the office could team them with these easier cottons.

Colour

After selecting the fabric, consider the colour. All men need a variety of shirt colours for different occasions in order to create the desired impressions on their audiences. Basic white – either pure, soft or ivory – will be appropriate for your most serious and authoritative shirt. Add to this some of the pastel options given for your colouring type, in Chapter Four. Pastels are more professional if they are almost indistinguishable from a white shirt – having a just discernible shade of some other colour. Stripes should not be worn when you need to give a presentation (too distracting) and they are best if subtle and not excessively bold. The British love bold stripes but few things give away a man's nationality quicker when travelling abroad than the coloured shirt, big stripes and stark white collar – here comes the Brit!

Collar Style and Fit

Collar selection is important for men who don't have standard necks and faces. That is, for very thin men with long skinny necks, collars that have narrow spreads (are close together) or are very long and pointed, emphasize the very features they wish to minimise. They are better in wide collars that 'break up' their length and create some width where needed. Conversely, men with very full faces and/short necks, especially thick ones, are better in narrow collars rather than cutaways or ones with a wide spread. Also, button-down collars are 'easier' on a full neck. Their softer fabric, usually Oxford cloth, is more forgiving on rolls of extra flesh. Tab collars are for chaps with average necks who like to show off their knots.

Some countries have a greater variety of collar shapes and bands (that is, in relation to the actual height of the collar). If your neck size is a problem and you can't easily find the options you need, consider investing in custom-made shirts. You can save money on other things but it is well worth spending whatever you must to create the most flattering line nearest your face.

In choosing your shirts the emphasis should be on a good fit and smart finish. Men who are uninterested in shirts are so usually because theirs don't fit them properly and hence they don't enjoy them. If a collar is uncomfortable, with skin sagging over the top, it is too tight. Either you bought the wrong size, the shirt has shrunk or you have expanded! But many men continue to buy their shirts too small because they haven't bothered to be re-measured although they may well know they have changed in shape (e.g. from weight-training or from putting on extra pounds). A too-large shirt is equally disastrous. If there is too much room when it is buttoned-up, you will look ill. There should be just enough room for you to fit one finger inside the collar or movement of about a quarter of an inch.

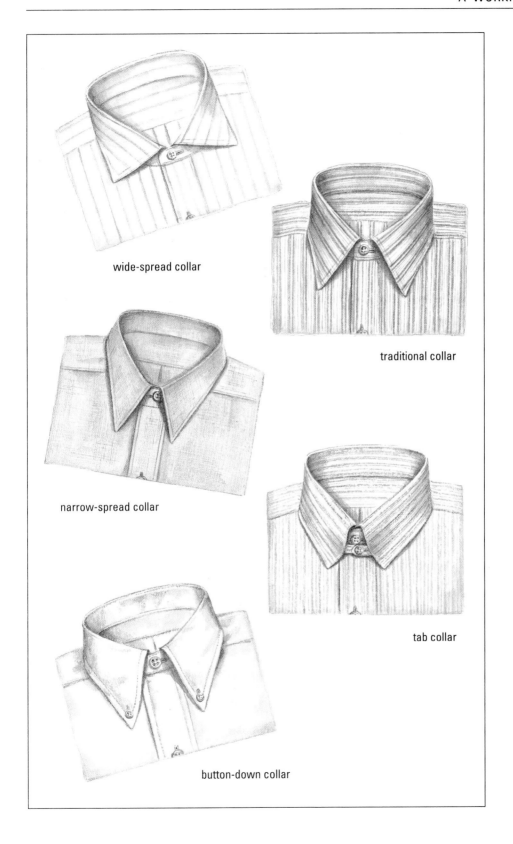

wide-spread collar

traditional collar

narrow-spread collar

tab collar

button-down collar

Make sure that your tie balances with your shirt collar. For a standard business collar, the preferred knot is the half-Windsor. When tied, the points of the collar should not stand out (they often do on cheaper shirts). If the knot looks too bulky or too small, then the fabric and/or the width of the tie is inappropriate. The cutaway collar was originally made for the fuller Windsor knot but looks acceptable with the finer half-Windsor knot (page 88).

Cuffs

Shirt cuffs can add variety as much as the colour or weave of your shirts. The basic two styles are the single or barrel, with one or two buttons, or the double or French cuff. The latter is far more elegant and a status symbol of a successful man; they cost more but they give your image an edge. You can then sport cufflinks which will express your personality and achievements better than any single-cuff shirt could hope to do. But avoid wearing single cuffs that pose as double cuffs, that is, the ones that have both buttons and a slit to enable you to wear cuff-links. They don't work and look ridiculous.

If you would like to try double cuffs but don't want to make the added investment of cufflinks, try a pair of simple but colourful silk knots. But if you really want to project success, invest in simple cufflinks in gold, silver, mother-of-pearl or a subtle-coloured stone such as onyx. Don't spoil your image by sporting juvenile designs, including 'wacky' plastic ones.

Also, remember to show a quarter-of-an-inch of cuff if wearing single cuffs (below right), and half-an-inch of double cuffs. Showing no cuff extending below your jacket sleeves — a 1980s trend with European suits — looks dreadful (below left).

left: No cuff is naff

right: A bit of cuff shows class

Pockets

The smartest business shirts never have a breast pocket, though many men like such a pocket because they can load them up with pens, cigarette cases and other odds and ends. Nothing pegs you as a back-room boy better than a shirt with a full pocket straining under the exertion. If your shirts have pockets, never use them (Americans please take note).

TIES

Here is one item of clothing that you wear daily to project your personality. A tie tells the world if a man is on his way up, if he has arrived or if he is on his way out.

If you wear someone else's choice around your neck all day – like that of the wonderful woman in your life – you are projecting qualities that aren't yours. A man must choose his own ties. If in doubt about combining colours and patterns consult the top salesman at a shop selling good ties, but don't let him or anyone else make the final selection. Take your time, selecting what *you* like best.

For business, choose ties of good quality silk that actually hold a knot. The more substantial the tie in weight the better able it is to do the job. Don't assume that in stressing a weighty tie I necessarily mean choose a thick silk. It has more to do with the construction, the lining of the tie than the silk itself. However, many 'designer' ties in beautiful colours and patterns sold today are of such thin silk or a light 'momme' (weight measurement of silk) that their lives are limited to a matter of months.

The lining should be of a good quality wool; you should be able to open the back of the tie to inspect its quality. If you can't, reject that tie. The silk itself should have been cut on the bias to allow it to lie flat and hang straight. Check if yours is, by hanging it by the narrow end to see if it falls straight. If it doesn't, and curls around instead, then you've picked up a poorly con-structed tie that would annoy you every time you wore it. Put it back on its rack and pass on!

The best ties are handmade in Italy, where tie-making is still a thriving cottage industry using mainly female outworkers for the task of sewing them together. You can tell if a tie is handmade by the discreet loop of thread hanging just inside the narrow end of the tie. If you pull it very gently, you will see it bunch up – proving that it has been hand sewn. Smooth out the tie again but do *not* cut this thread or the tie will fall apart. I had one client whose wife always did this and he couldn't understand why his ties never lasted very long.

The width of a tie should balance with the lapels of your suit. So if you have bought new suits recently but your ties date back several years, it is time for a few new ones. Also, your ties should be in balance with your build both in size and in pattern. Men who are slightly built should avoid large patterns, Windsor knots and wider ties. Large men require boldness in patterns, knot and width.

The ideal knot for most business suits, shirt collars and physiques is the half-Windsor. Here's how to do it:

The half-Windsor knot

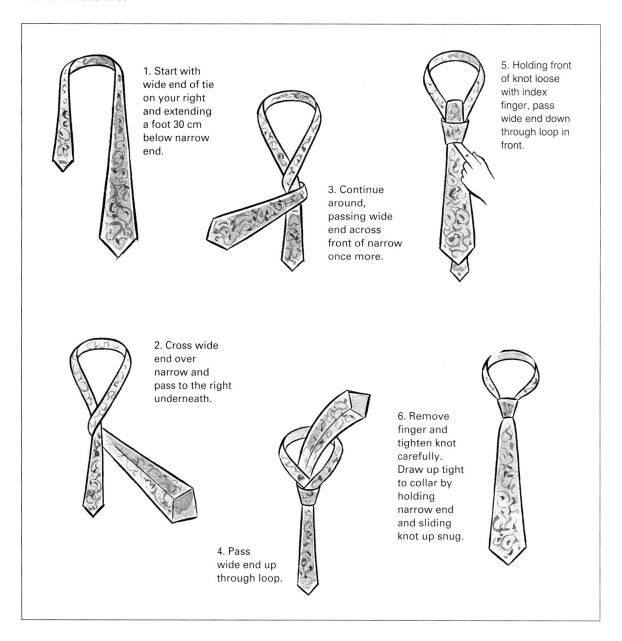

1. Start with wide end of tie on your right and extending a foot 30 cm below narrow end.

2. Cross wide end over narrow and pass to the right underneath.

3. Continue around, passing wide end across front of narrow once more.

4. Pass wide end up through loop.

5. Holding front of knot loose with index finger, pass wide end down through loop in front.

6. Remove finger and tighten knot carefully. Draw up tight to collar by holding narrow end and sliding knot up snug.

Bow Ties are for men who have the personality to carry them off. All men need a few to wear with their Dinner Jackets but also try wearing them with a smashing waistcoat (in lieu of a jacket) for social occasions where you don't need to look too formal. The best advice for tying one is not to look in the mirror but to imagine you are tying a shoe lace. Finish the bow, *then* look into the mirror and straighten it up, as necessary. Here's how to do it:

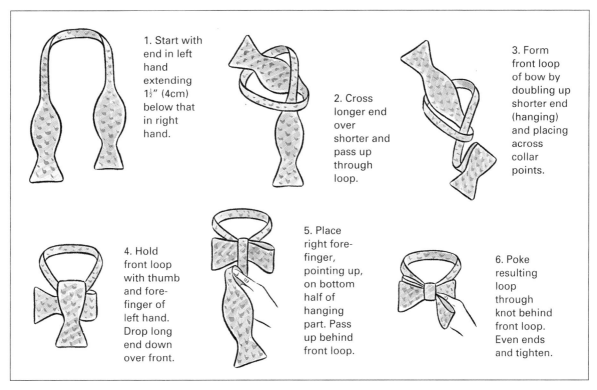

1. Start with end in left hand extending 1½″ (4cm) below that in right hand.

2. Cross longer end over shorter and pass up through loop.

3. Form front loop of bow by doubling up shorter end (hanging) and placing across collar points.

4. Hold front loop with thumb and forefinger of left hand. Drop long end down over front.

5. Place right forefinger, pointing up, on bottom half of hanging part. Pass up behind front loop.

6. Poke resulting loop through knot behind front loop. Even ends and tighten.

How to tie a bow tie

POCKET HANDKERCHIEFS

Silk pocket handkerchiefs can add a touch of style, individuality and creativity to a suit. But British, French and Italian men are more likely to wear a silk pocket handkerchief than other nationalities. Some men are put off by having seen them worn by some ghastly characters in American soaps; many conservative Americans opt only for the sharp-pointed white cotton hankie, which looks too safe and dated. Better to try silk and to use colour and patterns to enhance your suit, shirt and tie.

The key in selecting silk handkerchiefs, is to link the colours with your tie. A safe bet would be to wear a plain hankie in one of the dominant colours in your tie. More interesting would be to try a pattern, always different from your tie, that links the colours.

The best way to wear a pocket handkerchief is by using a technique taught to me by my friends at Turnbull & Asser on London's Jermyn Street:

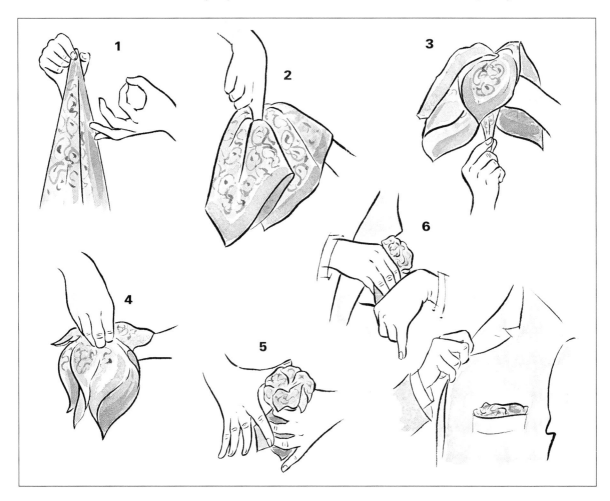

Step 1   Make a circle with your forefinger and thumb.

Step 2   Place the handkerchief, flat-out, over the circle and push the centre of it through the circle with your index finger.

Step 3   Pull gently from the centre point underneath, until just the point and border of the hankie are still exposed above your hand.

Step 4   With your free hand, grab the top of the handkerchief just above your circled finger, scrunching the whole outer circle of fabric together and release the hold of your circled forefinger and thumb.

Step 5   Now grab the fabric about 2 inches (5cm) below where you are holding, which you will see forms a sort of rosette with the fabric.

Step 6   Now twist the points or tail of the handkerchief, and plunge them into your suit breast pocket, with the rosette (hankie centre) remaining slightly exposed in gentle folds.

This technique, although requiring a certain amount of skill and care, allows your pocket handkerchief a certain natural panache. When worn any other way they can look contrived. Also, by using this technique, you are less likely to have the hankie sliding around or falling out. Give it a try.

SHOES

For too many men, shoes are an afterthought. Far from considering their shoe collection to be a wardrobe unto itself, as women do, men tend to hope that one or two good leather pairs along with a pair of trainers will cover all eventualities. Though, as always, I have met some memorable exceptions to the rule. One advertising client of mine wore lizard cowboy boots to work (thinking he was quite the bees-knees) and described clients in terms of shoes – the male staff at his building society as the 'grey plastic brigade', and his city bank as the 'brogue boys'. His taste in shoes was not exactly pol-ished but he vaguely realised their true importance. Shoes, like a man's tie, indicate status and success. What do you think your shoes say about you, about your position, attention to detail and professionalism?

In business, you have the option of the traditional lace-up shoes – the capped or brogue models – or the increasingly popular leather slip-on. A laced shoe is more professional and considered by many to be the only option when wearing a business suit. Certainly, in the most established professions, slip-on shoes are considered inappropriate.

Brogues come in a variety of styles and weight. For business, the heavy-soled double brogue (called wing-tips by the Americans), with its thick welts and elaborate punching, looks dated and out of place, particularly for men working internationally. Better to select the single or semi-brogues which provide a sleeker complement to your suits.

Slip-on shoes (loafers) are acceptable only if simple in style and of top quality leather. For business, avoid ones with gold bars (as in the Gucci-style shoe) or, indeed, any metal branding or design motifs. The simple tassle style is recommended only for men working in more relaxed business envi-ronments.

Shoes should be made only of leather both for the upper part and for the soles. Thick rubber soles only make you look like a 'backroom boy', regard-less of how comfortable they might be. Choose a calf-skin leather rather than suede, which is inappropriate unless you work in a rural environment. Good quality shoes also have a leather lining which allows your feet to 'breathe', and are most comfortable.

The most acceptable colour for shoes in business is black teamed with black, charcoal or navy socks. Oxblood, a maroon not brown shoe, is acceptable in many businesses, particularly those where slip-ons are not considered to be out of place. For the more fashion forward cities of Milan, Madrid, Düsseldorf and Paris, which approve brown-toned, olive, aubergine and other wonderful new shades being used in men's suiting, charcoal-brown shoes of the best quality are also possible. Avoid light colours or trendy 'colour-colours' like moss green or a true blue which sometimes sneak in among the offerings in men's shoe stores.

Caring for your shoes

Good quality shoes can last for years, provided you care for them well. Here are a few tips to ensure their longevity.

- Immediately after wearing, clean your shoes and polish if needed. When the leather is still warm, it absorbs polish much better, giving a deeper, more long-lasting shine. Polish underneath (in the arch) as well as on top.

- Allow each pair of shoes to rest for at least 36 to 48 hours after wearing.

- Store your shoes on shoe trees (plastic at minimum; wood at best) to prevent curling toes and creasing uppers.

- Have your shoes repaired as soon as you begin to notice wear. Take them to a good cobbler who will resole and reheel with leather not plastic, and touch up any scuff marks.

SOCKS

If you take no pleasure in buying your socks then you are not wearing the quality you deserve. Socks today are available in excellent quality at very affordable prices. Choose only wool, wool and cotton or wool and silk blends, avoiding totally man-made fibres. Wearing a polyester sock is like sticking your feet into plastic bags before putting your shoes on. The discomfort is surpassed only by the odour that will knock you out when you take your shoes off, and in no time you could develop foot problems – athlete's foot just for starters. Natural fibres breathe, allowing the sweat to be absorbed by the atmosphere and your feet to remain cool throughout the day.

Dark, elegant neutrals are the best colours to complement your suits; choose from black, navy, charcoal or subtle, indistinguishable weaves. Bright colours, such as red or yellow, or loud patterns do not tell the world you are an interesting fellow, they just indicate that you are screaming for attention. White, needless to say, has no place in business (sorry, German, Dutch and Finnish friends).

Socks are widely available in short, medium and knee-length, but whatever your preference, be sure that they cover your least erogenous zone – those inches of hairy shins and calves that come into view whenever you cross your legs. Even if your shins and calves are *not* hairy, they are still best kept under cover.

Keep your least erogenous zone . . .   . . . covered!

BELTS AND BRACES

If your trousers have loops, then you need a belt. Even if you keep your jacket on most of the day, trousers simply will not hang as they should if you don't belt up. If your waistline fluctuates and many of your trousers slip southward to hip level then the result is anything but smart; a belt would make all the difference.

Business belts should be simple and elegant. Wear only quality leather in black, navy or oxblood. Save the hand-hammered crafted models for your jeans.

Braces are the answer for men who hate any feeling of tightness or constriction at the waist. But if you belong to this school of thought, it is best if your trousers are of a quality that has buttons sewn inside the waistline to accommodate button braces. If not, clip-on models are acceptable. The days of the bright braces are over; choose subtle colours and patterns that don't clash with your ties (particularly important when you take your jacket off). But don't play it so safe that you always wear a matching tie and braces combo which only tells others that you don't have the confidence to mix and match.

CHAPTER 8

ACCESSORIES

THESE finishing touches are just as important to your image as the more obvious items – your suits, shirts and ties, but all too often they are over-looked. As soon as the subject of accessories comes up (I have included glasses), most men get nervous; they consider accessories to be fussy extras, most of which one can do without. On the contrary, accessories are the nec-essary items you **use** every day – your watch, pens, attaché-case or brief-case, and eyeglasses (if required). If you buy any old style of watch, pens, carry-all, or even eyeglasses so long as they work, then you are saying to others that you are indifferent to quality, weak on details and don't care too much what you look like.

GLASSES

Eyeglasses can be both cosmetic and constructive. Cosmetically speaking, you can wear glasses – with clear lenses – to look more authoritative, more intelligent – even older. Lots of clever young chaps have discovered this trick and wear glasses simply for effect.

Whether you wear them for cosmetic or for practical reasons – and in the latter case find spectacles preferable to contact lenses – there are some simple guidelines to help you select a pair that will complement your fea-tures and face shape, and fit comfortably.

Selecting glasses requires team work between you and your ophthalmol-ogist or optician. For instance, you might have your heart set on a designer frame but if they are too flimsy to hold your prescribed lenses, they won't work.

Accessories are the necessary finishing touches of your image

The frames should follow your facial lines but not actually match your face shape. For example, round frames on a fellow with a full, round face look ridiculous. Aviator glasses on a rectangular face look severe and off-putting. The key is to select a shape to counterbalance your features, perhaps creating some sharpness on a round face; or softening a square or angular face.

The top of the frames should line up with your eyebrows, unless you are keen on trendy round frames which go inside the eyebrows. Otherwise, you get a busy-looking double-eyebrow effect which only detracts from your eyes.

Your eyes should be 'centred' in the lenses. The frames should not be wider than your face nor lower than the centre of your cheeks, that is not as low as your nostrils.

If you have a large nose, opt for a narrow or clear bridge (the connecting bar over the nose). Bridges that are dark, heavy or double make the nose appear larger. Some styles have low bridges which effectively 'shorten' the length of a long nose.

Avoid tinted lenses that create a sinister image. Even though they may be handy for working outside, it is better to keep your sunglasses for outdoors in bright light and wear clear spectacles for work, so that people can maintain all-important eye contact with you.

Be sure that the colour of the frames complements your colouring. If your colouring is strong so, too, should your glasses be. If your eyebrows are dark have deep coloured frames, such as tortoiseshell. Conversely, if your hair and eyebrows are light, be careful not to overwhelm your face with very dark spectacles. Opt instead for a metal or light-coloured plastic; perhaps mottled grey or tan. Fun coloured frames are acceptable only in more relaxed companies or as a spare/weekend pair.

JEWELLERY

Less is best when it comes to wearing jewellery in a business environment. Sure, some men wear bracelets, necklaces and ear-rings, deluding themselves that they are expressing their uniqueness but, in fact, what they are doing is putting off 99.9 per cent of their colleagues and customers.

Rings should be limited to two, maximum; say, perhaps, a signet ring and a wedding band. Tie-bars and tie-pins come in and go out of fashion. Wear them only when they are 'in' and not merely because they have proved an efficient way to keep your tie out of your soup. Polish up your eating skills instead.

Medallions, gold chains, tribal wood carvings and the like belong with your casual wardrobe. Never wear them to a business occasion.

Brooches, pins and buttons are the quirks of other men. Only if worn to convey your support for a particular, time-limited event (for example, a charitable appeal or political campaign) will they be understood and acceptable to most people. Be careful of anything else, except in the most relaxed and informal business environment.

WATCHES

I do a 'watch inspection' during all of my men's seminars. If yours is made of plastic, rubber or diamonds or more colourful than your ties, or it bleeps or makes alarm noises, or is so high tech that you can't even figure out the time, then it's hurting your image. Whatever price you are prepared to pay, keep it simple.

Non-digital faces are the most elegant with a simple calfskin, mock-croc or metal strap, that will not constantly catch on your cuffs. Look for a design in which the glass is flush with the frame – raised glass faces soon become very scratched, making it difficult to tell the time, and looking unattractive.

It isn't simply a matter of having the glass replaced either. Most jewellers will only arrange this if you agree to have the watch serviced at the same time, and that involves leaving your watch with them for three or more weeks. Also avoid solid hunks of black – in face and strap – which always look cheap whatever they cost. Select one that will look great at the office as well as at weekends.

PENS

I bet you could describe what each of your closest colleagues uses to write with in meetings. Men are usually more particular about their pens and pencils than women and notice what others use.

Disposable pens should be used only at your desk, or when working at home. For meetings with clients/customers, peers or supervisors use a quality ball-point or fountain pen to impress. Sign all your letters with a fountain pen, to convey that you are a man who has taken time to read your correspondence carefully and you value what you sign. As maddening as fountain pens can be for those of us who write faster than the speed of light, they show deliberation and professionalism: two attributes you always want to

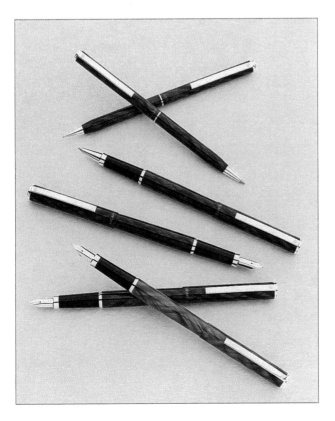

project when in the company of others in business. 'Topping and Tailing' correspondence, and hand-written 'thank-yous', are often well received by clients and customers in an age of word-processors and mailshots.

ATTACHÉS/BRIEF-CASES

Second only to your suit, your attaché or brief-case says who you are – your position, your status, your image, and it is indispensable for every successful man.

If you take work home or travel extensively you obviously need one that allows ample storage. But be smart; don't overload it just for effect or because you are too disorganised to file things away. After years of overstressing their arms and shoulders with an unnecessarily heavy attaché many men end up with at best a 'dropped arm' (always requiring adjustment in their suits – see Chapter Six) or, at worst, bursitis of the shoulder. If necessary, have two cases: one large pilot's case for weekend work and travel, and a slimmer attaché or brief-case for daily use.

Leaner attachés which carry the essentials are all that most men need – a few files, a newspaper, diary, pens, spare pad, etc. Some have well-designed retractable handles for greater versatility in use. Whatever the style, check that the handles are comfortable in use – some of the less well-padded ones cut into your hand – and quickly deteriorate. Narrow leather files are only for popping to meetings internally and convey 'lightweight' status: 'I'm just the note-taker', when travelling outside. However, if you are in a team, the lack of an attaché at meetings confers status and identification as the team leader.

The old-fashioned, two-handled brief-case is best left to solicitors or absent-minded professors who must lug around their lives with them.

Back-packs and shoulder bags are seen more frequently now, especially with younger men who prefer the easy practicality of lightweight carry-alls. By all means use one for travel to and from the office but never use it for an important meeting. Although attachés come in all forms of plastic, canvas, metal and fabric the only acceptable material to complement the status of a successful man is leather in a rich dark colour like black, tortoiseshell, mahogany, burgundy, charcoal or navy.

CHAPTER 9

GROOMING FOR SUCCESS

THERE'S a lot to be said for good grooming. It doesn't cost much but it pays dividends, and it only requires a little effort every day. If you don't make time to groom yourself in the morning, you – and more important, others – will regret it all day.

Being well-groomed – clean, polished and presentable – shows respect for yourself and everyone you work with. You might not be able to afford the best wardrobe in town but you can look successful if you bother with your grooming, as outlined below.

YOUR BODY

All men require a daily bath or shower. In fact, anyone who lives in a town or city environment could benefit from the same treat both morning and evening. The main concern is with the level of your perspiration; which we all exude in varying amounts and degrees of pleasantness.

You perspire according to the body heat you generate (again, that's individual) from dashing around, and the environment in which you work. When you get nervous, are under pressure, you sweat more. Certain foods such as Indian curries and Chinese Szechuan also activate the sweat glands. If you know they trigger this reaction in you, try to avoid them on work days, and at business lunches.

Everyone benefits from using a deodorant. These are now available as sprays, puff-ons, wet and dry roll-ons, and in a variety of strengths. Unscented versions are also widely available. Heavy perspirers are also recommended to use a deodorant soap.

Wear fresh under-clothing and a fresh shirt every day. If you are clean, but wear day-old (or heaven forbid, older) under-clothes or shirts, you will get new perspiration working with stale perspiration, which causes *odour*. Do a regular sniff test on the armpits of your jackets to detect any build-up of perspiration. Regular airing will help to freshen them but dry cleaning is the only way to remove old perspiration. Even so, try to keep dry cleaning to the minimum, to sustain the longevity of your suits.

Aftershaves and Colognes

The right scent can be a marvellous boost to your image, but if you get it wrong you will leave lasting and negative impressions on everyone you meet. So it is important to choose one that is compatible with your body chemistry. Don't be beguiled into impulse buying by high-pressure advertising.

You might be familiar with the variety of smells on offer in the department stores, and perhaps you have a tried and tested favourite. But do you know how others like being around it? What works with effect, after hours with the opposite sex, usually sends the wrong signals to business colleagues during the day. Generally speaking, an aftershave or cologne suitable for office wear will be subtle, light and fresh-smelling. Use a tester in the shop or store before buying, and ask for a second opinion if you are still in doubt.

Even then, play safe and don't try out your new buy when you have an important meeting or interview; my advice is, when uncertain, do without altogether. Nothing beats that 'just out of the shower' fresh, clean smell. A good deodorant soap like Zest, Shield or Fresh, often leaves just enough of a hint of a nice scent to please everyone around you.

YOUR FACE

Men, like women, require a basic skin-care regime to maintain a healthy complexion. Twice daily you need to cleanse, tone and moisturise your face to remove grime and pollution.

- Choose a gentle foaming cleanser that will lather up with warm water to help remove grime and natural sweat. Pay particular attention to your cheeks, nose and forehead, which don't get cleansed as regularly as your beard area.

- Splash your face 10 times with warm water to remove the excess cleanser. Now shave.

- After shaving, use a gentle toner, without alcohol, to remove all excess shaving cream and cleanser (there will be plenty of residue).

- Then use an unperfumed moisturiser with UVA and UVB sunscreen to retain the moisture in your skin, as well as to seal your skin from airborne pollutants. All the moisturiser should be absorbed (3 to 5 minutes) before applying aftershave. If you've never used a moisturiser before, bear in mind that a little goes a long way, and that it should be applied as a very thin 'film' on your skin's surface – don't rub it in! Your skin will absorb it more efficiently and beneficially if you let it get on with the task.

If your skin isn't your best feature, also consider your diet. Eating more raw vegetables, and fresh fruit, and drinking a litre of mineral water daily should bring about an enormous, visible improvement within a short time. Any form of exercise that causes you to sweat generously also serves to deep clean your pores naturally and give the skin a glow more becoming than an artificial, sunbed tan.

If you have a problem with eczema or acne, don't try to treat it cosmetically. Consult a dermatologist. There are now excellent products available only on prescription but highly effective. The occasional spot is best left alone (i.e. avoid popping or squeezing); invest in a medicated cosmetic stick that blends in with your own skintone and use it at the first sign of trouble. (Most good chemists stock these cosmetic sticks.)

Unwanted Hair

One eyebrow

No one looks attractive or clean with one eyebrow; that is, one unbroken line that extends across the top of your eyes and the bridge of your nose like a fuzzy caterpillar. Clean out between the brows to define both eyes separately (see opposite page, top). Try tweezers if there are only a few hairs or use a depilatory cream or wax to remove heavier patches. Most good beauty salons (unisex) as well as top barbers will sort this out for you if you can't bring yourself to do it on your own. Electrolysis is another more permanent option which you might like to discuss at a beauty salon that provides this service.

Thick brows

If your brows are very thick, they can be a striking feature but only if they are kept under control. Consider having yours trimmed if they stick out too far. The aim is to retain the fullness but minimise the amount of unruly, stray hairs. This is done with a fine comb and pair of sharp scissors; a good barber or hairdresser will be happy to do this for you every time you have a trim if you so wish.

left: Stray hairs can make you look unkempt

right: A little effort makes you look more polished

Fuzzy nostrils and ears

This problem seems to strike just when you are about to have your mid-life crisis, as if that wasn't enough. But few things are more distracting to other people than hairs that extend from your nostrils. If this is a problem for you, invest in a specially designed pair of nose scissors and – with all due care – learn to trim them for yourself (this is not a job for the barber or your partner).

Remember that you are viewed from the side more often than face-on. So, if your ears are 'woolly', they might not bother you but can be a turn-off to others. Give yours a thorough wash and then ask your partner or your mother to tidy them up with a fine pair of nail scissors.

Heavy Beard Line

Some men have a heavy beard line, and no matter how often they shave, their chins never look as clean shaven as their fairer haired colleagues.

To minimise the effect of a heavy beard line, opt for white or pink shirts rather than blue, which will emphasise any six o'clock shadow.

left: The wrong-coloured shirt exacerbates a heavy beard line

right: Get your colours right to look better groomed

Moustaches and Beards

Men who are clean-shaven have a better chance of getting a job, and being widely and readily accepted in business. A sweeping statement perhaps, but many decision-makers have such negative attitudes to men with beards that it has to be noted, even if what I write next seems to be in direct contradiction.

For men who have insignificant chins, I always *recommend* growing a beard. A strong jawline or chin is considered masculine. So, chaps who have been short-changed by nature can 'create' a chin with a beard; it gives definition and shape where there isn't any naturally.

If you are more senior in your career or have total confidence in your position and like a beard or moustache, go for it. I am all for breaking down silly prejudices where they exist and this one against beards and moustaches is a good example of one whose days should be numbered. Keep yours well-trimmed: it would be best to keep your neck clean-shaven and limit the beard to your face and chin. Be honest about the quality, if it grows in thin and patchy, it looks awful. You'd be better to revert to being clean-shaven.

left: A beard in business puts many people off

right: A clean-shaven face is more professional as well as approachable

Warts and Moles

The cleaner your face, the better you look. I've suggested that you cover any blemishes that pop-up from time to time but more permanent distractions, like warts and moles, can be removed medically. Consult your doctor, who will be able to prescribe a lotion or paste for any warts, and refer you to a hospital for surgical removal of any unsightly or protuberant moles.

Some moles pass as 'beauty marks', not because they are necessarily beautiful but because they are small, have no hairs growing out of them and aren't excessively three dimensional. In such instances, it is best to leave well alone.

YOUR TEETH

Clean, healthy teeth and gums should be a priority in your daily grooming. You should brush three times – yes, after lunch, especially. So many people have odorous breath in the afternoon because of what they have eaten at lunchtime: garlic, curry, cheese, fish, wine, coffee, are just some of the worst causes. At least once a day, after cleaning your teeth, use dental sticks or floss to make sure you really have removed all food debris from areas where your toothbrush cannot reach. This will also help to keep your gums firm and a healthy pink colour.

Also visit a dental hygienist 3 times a year to treat your teeth to a professional cleaning and polishing. Even though you brush daily, teeth can become stained by food and drink (especially tea, coffee and red wine), smoking as well as from ageing. A professional cleaning can make a dramatic improvement. The hygienist will also advise you on the state of your gums – their health is vital to the long-term health and durability of your teeth.

Many leading politicians and business people have had teeth that detracted from their appearance before corrective dentistry. Prime Ministers Thatcher and Wilson are famous examples. If your teeth cause you any embarrassment, do consider seeing a recommended cosmetic dentist who can help straighten, whiten or fill gaps to give you more confidence in your appearance and powers of communication. Some dental treatments that can work wonders include:

Whitening   You can be fitted with a bleaching mould which, worn for an hour a day for 6 weeks, produces dramatic results.

Brown gums   A sign of gingivitis (gum disease) that requires immediate attention if you are to save your teeth. Healthy gums are pink and they don't bleed when you brush your teeth.

Ugly fillings   Can be replaced with white porcelain to match your teeth.

Dark teeth   Can be covered with porcelain veneers matched to the colour of your other teeth.

Crowns   A broken or decayed tooth can be filed down and capped or even wholly replaced with a porcelain tooth on a post, provided the root is intact and healthy.

Dentures   Necessary for some people, e.g. who have lost their teeth through accidents. They can look natural if fixed permanently in to the gums as implants.

YOUR HANDS

Your hands are always on display, particularly when dealing one-to-one or in small groups, whether shaking hands in greeting, passing around notes, using a flip-chart while making a presentation – you use them a lot without even thinking about it. In the same way, you might not be aware of how nice some of your colleagues' hands are, but you certainly notice who has terrible ones – and I'm not referring here to their shapes. We are not all blessed with shapely hands, but they should be smooth and well-manicured.

If you feel you are 'all thumbs' when it comes to doing your own manicure ask your partner for help or organise it through your hairdresser/barber. After a few professional treatments you should be able to do it yourself.

Daily Care

- Soak your hands in warm soapy water (that is, if you shower instead of bathe), then clear any trapped dirt from underneath your nails.

- Rub a little cuticle cream in around the nails if they are brittle and tend to peel or flake.

- Use a hand cream to keep your skin soft and smooth.

Weekly Care

- Soak your hands in warm soapy water.

- Gently push back the cuticles with another of your nails, a wooden manicure stick or scissors – go carefully if you use these.

- File your nails into a natural squarish shape. A medium-grain emery board is easier on your nails than a steel file, unless you have particularly strong nails with no tendency to split.

- Buff the tips of your nails with a fine-grain emery board to give a really smooth finish and then polish your nails with a buffer, to promote an attractive sheen and healthy growth.

YOUR HAIR

We are discussing grooming and the place to begin is with cleanliness. You should wash your hair daily with a gentle shampoo designed for regular use. Check on the label. Even if your hair is dry, your scalp will benefit from removal of all the daily pollutants, just as your face and body do. The point is that your hair should never look as if it needs a wash, so gels that give that greasy, grunge effect are out.

Dandruff

If dandruff is a problem, try a medicated shampoo. Some sufferers find they need to change the shampoo every few months as dandruff seems to become immune to one treatment used for a longer period. Always rinse your hair thoroughly afterwards to remove all traces of shampoo.

Heavy and persistent dandruff could be a symptom of some dietary disorder, so it is worth consulting a trichologist. And, if you do use hair lacquer fairly regularly, check that this is always washed out thoroughly when you shampoo. Keep combs and hairbrushes scrupulously clean.

Keep a clothes brush in the office and dust down your shoulders once or twice a day; especially before an important meeting. Obviously, darker colours show the dandruff more; if dandruff is a perennial problem, stick to medium-charcoal grey suits.

The Cut

Obviously, this is a very personal choice. And some of us like to experiment with new styles while others are happy with the same basic cut year after year (and still look wonderful).

Don't allow yourself to be swayed by what others are wearing, find a cut that suits your face shape, build and lifestyle. To compliment your face, don't repeat its shape in your hairstyle, that is, if you have a very round face and thick hair that is cut for fullness at the sides, your face will look chubby, not just round. A good hairdresser should be able to advise you if you're not sure which style is best for you.

Remember to check your grooming from front, back and sides. If between visits to the barber you need a trim around the sideburns and ears *(right)*, get a friend to oblige. The back of your neck should be regularly defuzzed too.

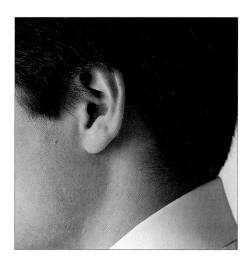

A good cut should also complement your build or size. For example, a big guy looks scary with a closely-shaven head. Conversely, a slight man looks overwhelmed by too much hair. Balance is the key.

Receding hair will be less noticeable if you stick to a shorter hairstyle. Long, straggly tendrils at the neck and sides only serve to emphasise the sparsity on top. Any attempt to create an illusion of luxuriant top growth by growing side hair long and combing it up and over looks odd – and is quickly devastated by the slightest mischievous wind. Keep it short; it is the only way to look neat and polished and to exhibit your remaining mane at its best.

Thinning Hair looks healthy and fuller if cut in layers and also kept short. Towel dry your hair after washing and use a little mousse (size of a golf ball), evenly applied, to add volume.

Despite the claims in the back of men's magazines, to date there is no cure for baldness. A huge industry of hair replacements, wigs, weaving and transplants simply plays upon the insecurities of men unable to deal with this natural process. In all the years I have worked with men who have sought help, I have rarely found one who was completely satisfied with his efforts to overcome natural balding despite having spent hundreds, even thousands, of pounds. Men's hairpieces, unless customised and made by the most skilful, are recognisable a mile off. Other men are uncomfortable with chaps wearing toupées and can get so distracted when dealing with them that the hairpiece can actually interfere with communication.

If you are balding, accept the course of nature and keep your hair short for best effect.

Thick hair requires skilful cutting if it is to look real. Yes, many men blessed with a full head of hair look as if they are wearing wigs because they don't get it cut by a specialist. If this applies to you look no further than the best salon near you which also does women's hair (sorry, but it is mostly barbers who are responsible for the artificial look).

Such hair needs more than just a regular thinning. It also requires some clever scissor work to create a sense of movement. Even though your thick hair may rarely blow in the wind it can look more 'real' after a session with a clever stylist.

Curly hair also needs special attention. If the shape isn't right you can look clownish and ill-kempt. Best advice is to keep the cut short, close to the head but not too short for the world (especially women!) not to be able to appreciate your curls. It is time for a cut when the curls start tickling your ears or ring round your collar.

The last but just as important factor you need to consider in getting the right cut, is your lifestyle. How much time can you – or are you prepared to – spend on making your hair look nice each day. If you are an under-two-minute flick with the brush and comb chap, don't get a style that requires lots of attention with gels and mousses, blow-drying and clever tricks with brushes. You simply won't keep it up, so you will not look your best.

Long Hair

Some men get attached to their long hair during their carefree teens and find it hard to give it up and compromise their image for the conventional workplace. But long hair is acceptable in a number of industries – such as fashion, the media, marketing and advertising – and it can be a real asset to a man's image, if his mane looks healthy, manageable and attractive.

Long hair worn in business is distracting and off-putting. On men, loose locks almost always look wild and unkempt as most men aren't willing to put in the time required on grooming their hair. To win wider acceptance of your long hair, wear a neat ponytail and remember the following tips:

- Make sure your hair is clean every day as longer hair on men will be scrutinised more closely than shorter hair.

- Wear your ponytail tight, not sliding out of a loose band

- Use plain black or brown hairbands and avoid coloured ones

- Don't use elastic bands as they ruin your hair.

- Keep your neck and side-burns trimmed and as cleanly-shaven as your beardline.

  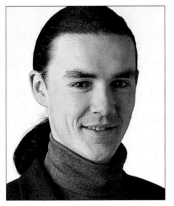

unkempt   well-groomed

The Treatments

Your hair can look terrific no matter whether you spend two minutes or 20 minutes on it in the morning, provided you find the right treatments to compensate for what Mother Nature hasn't provided.

Anyone's hair – whether a man or a woman – can be made to look fuller, curlier, shinier, more colourful than it is naturally. If you haven't found out the options to make your hair more interesting as well as easier to care for consult a different hairdresser, preferably one recommended to you by someone whose hair always looks good. Soft perms, highlighting, low-lighting, semi-permanent rinses or permanent tints are options for all men these days – why let women have all the cosmetic advantages? Lots of young male athletes have clearly got the message. And just consider how many actors literally transform themselves simply by changing the cut, styling and colour of their hair.

The local pharmacy offers a wide choice of preparations such as mousses, gels and sprays that should find a place on everyone's bathroom shelves.

- Mousses are used mainly to add volume and control before blow-drying the hair into shape.

- Gels are great if used in moderation; just squeeze a dot into your hand, then rub your hands together before brushing them through your hair, spreading the gel evenly. It will then help your hair stay in place without looking set. Gels are not just effective but also look more natural than sprays.

- Hairsprays are very efficient but if just sprayed all over the top create a helmet-effect. Much better to lightly spray underneath sections of the hair to create some volume then apply a final easy, fine spray at the front. Hair is meant to move. So be sure you don't overdo it.

FIT FOR SUCCESS

IN THE last few years there has been a re-definition of what it takes to project success. Not only do you need to look smart by wearing appropriate clothes of good quality but you must also look healthy. Being fit and 'in shape' have become a metaphor for being in control of yourself – and your career. Men who are in control of themselves are in charge of their jobs; they are the successful ones.

Sedentary readers may be ready to flip to another section. 'Spare me another lecture about losing weight, taking up jogging or pumping iron. I am too busy and, quite frankly, just beyond it.' The weak of flesh and spirit can take heart, however, because the experts no longer recommend vigorous, sweaty pursuits as the only way to tone-up. Indeed, if you're really out of shape, they can be dangerous. The best results – most long-lasting and effective for the uninitiated – are just small changes to your sedentary lifestyle that can both strengthen your vital organs, your heart especially, and make you look more alert and feel more energetic.

FAT IS A DISCRIMINATORY ISSUE

How do you define someone who looks unhealthy? The scales don't tell the complete story. Many large men who, according to slimming experts, are 'overweight' are very fit and healthy but technically do not conform to standards of desirable weights for certain heights and bone structures. A person with an unhealthy image does not have to be overweight; he can be skinny and puny instead. It is just that the overweight are considered to be more responsible for their condition. It is reasoned that they probably ate themselves into their state and they are judged harshly if they don't get themselves out of it and into a condition valued as 'ideal'.

Like it or not, overweight people are also discriminated against at work. In a survey we at CMB conducted of Britain's top 200 companies in 1992, personnel and financial directors ranked looking 'fit and healthy' as the second key factor in hiring people (just behind a smart appearance). They defined 'fit' as trim and not overweight. American clinical psychologist Sarah Gilbert says, 'Research suggests that there are some people who think that fat people are more stupid than other people, less intelligent, more sloppy, less organised.'

A widely-held perception in business and public life is that the overweight just let themselves go, that they can't control themselves. If they can't control themselves then how can they be expected to deliver on the job. They won't be as exacting or as persevering as their fitter colleagues. If they can't even plan what they eat to get their weight under control, how can they be relied on to plan anything else?

The prejudice goes on. For example, when considering testing assignments further up the ladder, the boss may well send someone else on an important sales call or presentation because the overweight person's image is felt to reflect badly on the company. Therefore he loses out; his career gets blocked. Many times I have discussed the fitness (or lack thereof) of staff with their managers. They whisper behind closed doors that they can't rely on Mr X and worry if he can handle the pace of the job. If deciding between two competent people on whom to send overnight to New York on the 'Red-Eye' for the morning presentation, you can bet that if one is very overweight the person who is in better shape will be perceived as better for this exacting assignment.

Unlike sex and race discrimination, there is no legislation about discrimination against overweight people, except in the state of California where it is illegal to discriminate in hiring just on the basis of how a person looks – that covers the unattractive as well as the overweight. If you don't look healthy and are substantially overweight you will probably be subjected to discrimination. You will miss out on potential job advancement, new opportunities and, possibly, the pay you deserve because you don't have what the business world today considers a Successful Image. The right clothes can help but they can't hide a body that most consider only in pejorative terms.

TAKING CONTROL

You know what it takes to be healthy. You don't need a lecture on eating sensibly. You are bombarded with dieting advice by television, magazines and newspapers. But if you think that your diet is poor, that you eat all the wrong things at the wrong times, or that you simply eat too much and don't know where to begin to put it right, then see a qualified dietician. Your doctor should be able to refer you to one. Before your appointment eat as normal and keep an accurate diary of everything you put into your mouth for a week. This will show what, how, and when you eat during the working week and at weekends. Such a record is very revealing and, in itself, a sobering incentive to start a diet; importantly it also guides a dietician in helping you develop the necessary remedial eating plan. With a diet in hand, you then need an assessment of your activity level to see if you get enough exercise to keep and to look fit.

If it has been a while since you had a complete physical examination, and you don't know exactly how fit you are for your age, it's time to book an appointment with your doctor or a fitness assessment clinic – a medical one, not your local gym. Most private health insurers have these clinics, and you don't necessarily have to be a member of their scheme in order to book a fitness assessment, obviously at a price. But consider this to be one of the best investments in your life.

FIT YET UNFIT

The American fitness guru, Dr Kenneth Cooper (the man who coined 'aerobics') recommends a fitness stress test as part of any annual physical check-up. This is where you are hooked up to an electrocardiogram while carrying out some form of exercise like walking, riding an exercise bicycle or running on a treadmill. This is the only way you can find out if a heart attack is on the way. Through this test doctors can see if any of the arteries to the heart are under strain or blocked. Cooper has had fitness-freaks take this test who would have been dead in a matter of weeks had he not picked up the blockages on the ECG. After 40, you should have this test done every 2 years, according to Cooper.

After a good physical check-up, it's time to analyse your activity level and develop a fitness programme to suit your lifestyle. The good news is that you don't need to take out an expensive Health Club membership to get your fitness under control. You can build it into your life by changing your behaviour throughout the regular workday. It is the extent to which you move your body and are active throughout the day that determines your fitness as much as any regular workout programme. Walking, climbing stairs, lifting and carrying things rather than resorting to all the modern conveniences available to avoid activity, like cars, escalators and lifts or porters, can keep you as fit as you need to be.

Aerobic exercises, like jogging, cycling or swimming, are the most efficient for improving and maintaining general body-fitness

If you aren't in a hurry to transform your body into an Arnold Schwarzenegger or a Carl Lewis you are advised to take exercise slowly but to carry out some moderate activity for longer periods. So rather than the ten minutes dash around the park in the morning, walk 20 or 30 minutes to the office (get off the train a stop or two early or park your car farther away). Do this three or four days a week and you will have a fitter body in six months. To see bigger changes sooner you will need to diversify your activity to include some anaerobic work (e.g. muscle strengthening through weight training), along with more advanced aerobic activities like jogging, cycling or swimming.

Aerobic activities are the key to becoming, looking and feeling fit. Dr Kenneth Cooper, who wrote all the seminal works on aerobics and now directs the Cooper Aerobics Institute in Dallas, has studied the correlation between death and fitness among businesspeople who came to his clinic for health checks. The greatest number of fatalities were among those who took no exercise at all. However, the people who took 'some exercise' had a significantly improved lifespan over those who did 'nothing at all'.

So with just a little effort you can not only look and feel better but you can last longer. Fitness helps you fight off the degenerative processes of ageing like heart disease, high blood pressure, and stiff joints. You can have a say in how fast you age. The fit and healthy in their forties can have the vitality of sedentary specimens ten to fifteen years younger, and often have even more energy. So fitness can help the insecure middle-aged who are threatened with younger talent vying for their jobs, by keeping them a few paces ahead – both literally and figuratively!

Walk Before You Run

Walking, a favoured pastime throughout Europe, is now a sport, and is the best exercise for the uninitiated. In America, walking clubs have popped up everywhere, hitting the streets and shopping malls alike. You don't need to spend money on anything special, but you do need sensible, supportive and comfortable shoes to make the most of walking and to encourage yourself to go for longer stints.

Walking is much safer than running and more practical for working people, because it is part of everyday life. But make sure you know 'how to walk', to get the most out of the activity. I am not being cute, suggesting that able-bodied men who regularly put one foot in front of the other don't know how to walk. It is just that shuffling along or walking all hunched up doesn't make the most of the exercise. Throw your shoulders back to allow your lungs to function fully. Next, thrust your pelvis forward – not artificially, just more than you normally would – to allow full movement of the hips; you want them to roll easily from side to side as you walk. It is preferable to walk unencumbered, letting your arms swing easily as you move. Consider using a backpack to carry your gear to and from the office (keeping your smart attaché in your desk for meetings throughout the day). See Chapter Eight.

Use your whole foot when you walk. Feel your toes, land heel first then roll your sole forward. Use your ankles. Stretch your stride. The longer the stride the greater the effort and the more muscles you stretch throughout your body. A good walk engages the whole body as well as your mind and, eventually, your spirit. If you build more walking into your day, into your life, you'll feel and look fitter in no time.

It's Got to be Fun

If you have any hope of getting and maintaining fitness, you must find an activity that you enjoy. What turns your mates on might be pure hell for you. Some men like solitary activity like running or cycling on their own. Others are truly social animals when it comes to exercise; they simply can't rely on themselves to develop and keep to a routine. If this is you, then select something that is relatively easy to organise and that you will actually look forward to doing with your friends and/or partner like tennis, squash or swimming.

Circuit Training has caught on not simply for its sociability but also for its efficiency as a pre-work or lunchtime activity. In 45 minutes you raise your pulse rate through initial aerobic activity (jogging, cycling, jumping jacks, sprints, etc.) and maintain it while varying anaerobic work on different muscle groups. Every two to three minutes you change your activity – knee bends, sit-ups, squats, leg-lifts, free-weights, press-ups, etc. – and run repeated circuits of exercise. It is fun, exhausting and competitive. You get stronger and noticeably fitter within a matter of weeks. The key is to schedule it in three times a week. One intensive workout weekly is a waste of time, both exhausting and foolhardy, and only beneficial in relieving guilt. Once you commit to being active, it's got to be on a regular basis, without long breaks in between, in order to see results in your body and fitness.

Boxing is another activity gaining in popularity. In California, both men and women flock to the rings to take out all the frustrations of the day. Like circuit training, boxing (wearing a head protector) is terrific for toning the muscles as well as strengthening the heart. Unlike other sports, you get vicarious thrills in punching your nemesis in the nose!

So look for a sport or activity that you might enjoy and that could become an integral part of your life. If the programme always depends on others, ask yourself if you aren't looking for an easy way out when they can't make it. Keep the organising to the minimum. If you can count on a weekly squash game with a reliable mate balance that with a circuit training at the gym and a long cycle ride at the weekend. Whatever it is, build it into your diary. Make it an appointment equal in importance to all the other major ones in your life and soon you will realise that exercise is your most important commitment every day, every week.

THAT BEAUTIFUL BUZZ

Just in case you need a final word of encouragement, exercise is beneficial not simply to help burn calories and to keep your weight down but research has shown that it also improves performance dramatically in areas as diverse as concentration, IQ, and muscle endurance (not to mention fertility and sexual performance!). Speak with any of your fit colleagues and ask them why they are so active and they will tell you it is for the *feeling* they get after activity that makes them keep it up – not to lose weight necessarily.

Go for that same feeling, that wonderful *buzz*. Anything bothering you before a good walk or a visit to the gym, evaporates within minutes. Exercise makes you think more clearly, it gets your worries into perspective. You can be tied-up in knots over a problem and find yourself laughing it off after a workout. No drink nor drug enables you to do that and still function – but exercise does!

CHAPTER 11

THE IMAGE OF YOUR VOICE

THE success of many politicians, actors and business people can be attributed to some extent to the quality of their voices. Think for a minute of the voices you admire. The radio breeds some splendid examples with whom we are all familiar: the BBC's morning news presenters Brian Redhead and Peter Hobday; the American writer and broadcaster, Garrison Keillor; and, Canadian, now British, DJ Diana Luke.

When we mention the names of some famous people you can immediately **hear** them ... Jeremy Irons, Eddie Murphy, Her Majesty The Queen, Marilyn Monroe, Richard Burton, Cilla Black, John Major. Their voices are distinctive and integral to their personalities. If Richard Burton had had John Major's voice would he have been such a successful actor? Would Mr Major's political fortunes be different if he could speak to us like Jeremy Irons or Richard Burton? Would Marilyn Monroe have been as sexy with Hillary Clinton's voice?

What impression does your voice leave with other people? Is your laugh in the memorable Eddie Murphy mode? Is your monotone more reminiscent of John Major?

Your voice accounts for 38 per cent of the impression you make on people; 55 per cent depends on how you look and behave and only 7 per cent on what you are saying (*Silent Messages*, Professor A. Mehrabian, University College Los Angeles). Don't think, however, that if you look, act and sound wonderful you can speak rubbish. Of course, you can't. But in business and politics we have to assume you know what you are talking about (or someone can back you up). It is more a question of how you sell your message. If you can't sell your ideas you can't succeed in business or public life.

A good voice enhances your professional stature as well as keeps your audience's attention when you speak. A bad voice at best bores and at worst irritates, thus undermining the rest of your image that you have worked so hard to develop.

IS YOUR VOICE IN-TUNE?

Think of your own voice. If any of the following problems apply to you when you get up and speak, then some work is required to improve your voice.

- You feel unnatural when speaking and hear a different voice, usually higher than your normal conversational tone.

- You're an adult but your voice sounds adolescent. Sometimes people ring you at home and ask to speak to your dad.

- People ask you to speak-up, even if you are speaking in a small gathering and everyone is well within ear-shot.

- You use 'fillers' when you speak: 'um', 'right', 'you know', 'and so forth'.

- You sound flat when speaking through a microphone.

- Your voice gets tired and your throat hurts after speaking for 15 or 20 minutes.

- You have a strong regional accent not widely understood. People often say, 'Excuse me, could you repeat that?'

- You finish sentences high as if you are asking a question when you are actually stating a fact.

- You don't sound authoritative.

- You simply don't like the sound of your voice!

Do Something About It!

You are not condemned for life to have an indifferent or poor voice. You can do something about it.

Your voice is mainly conditioned by your experience – how and where you grew up, where your parents were from, the schools you attended, the kids you hung around with. As an adult, other influences come into play – how much you have travelled, your colleagues at work and how they speak, the programmes you watch on television or listen to on the radio, your partner's voice.

Before reaching for the Yellow Pages to find a speech therapist, there are several things you can do to improve your voice that won't cost anything. Here's where to start.

1. Ask your friends and closest colleagues what, if anything, they like about your voice and what they find irritating. If they look a bit bemused tell them how you would like to sound. Here are some qualities you might be aiming for:

    Clarity, richness, sounding authoritative, colourful, energetic, commanding, pleasing, reassuring, confident, friendly, intelligent, natural, professional.

    Ask them if, in their opinion, you already have some of these qualities.

2. If he or she is approachable, consult your boss or supervisor, who has heard you speak, for an assessment on your voice and its effect. (You may earn some Brownie points for showing self-improvement initiative.)

3. Read out loud; try to be more expressive and improve your pronunciation, pace and modulation. You don't necessarily need an audience for this, but it would be helpful to have someone present who sympathises with your aim and will be honest in their opinion.

4. Read to children. They are the most honest audience you will ever get. If you keep their attention, you are doing well. If they start to fidget and stop listening, you've lost. Ask them if they like listening to you – and why. (One tip to bolster your chances: pick a good story, preferably something scary.)

5. Record your voice on to a tape recorder. Do short three minute 'speeches', pretending you are being interviewed on the radio on a subject about which you can speak off the cuff, for example the trip to work this morning; what you enjoyed about a recent film; describe your favourite restaurant. Analyse each of your 'performances' and aim to improve the next recording by what you learned on previous ones.

Don't erase the tape. Keep it as a record, to help you monitor your progress.

PREPARING FOR A PRESENTATION

So, you have worked to improve your voice and it's now time actually to get up and speak. Most presenters get nervous, so you are not alone. Here's what you need to do to control your nerves, and to allow your voice to project as best as possible.

Relax Your Body

The adrenalin is pumping through your body as you wait for your turn to speak. This is when you can tense-up from head to toe; and if the tension is really bad, your throat seizes up as well.

Try to exercise the night before or, better still, the morning of a big presentation. This should include a good aerobic workout like running, swimming or cycling, and some stretching exercises. Before you speak, go for a brisk walk wherever you can; around the block, up and down a few flights of stairs, through the lobby of the conference centre. Brisk movement before you begin speaking allows the adrenalin to release throughout your body rather than tense up your muscles making you paralytic, but don't overdo it and make yourself breathless.

Now Breathe

I know you have been doing this your whole life, but you might recall an occasion when you had to speak, or were about to be interviewed on TV or radio, when breathing became very difficult, strange and somewhat scary. You can never perform well if you are not breathing normally and naturally.

Your breathing controls the oxygen supply to your blood, which in turn feeds your brain which, I know you appreciate, must be engaged in order for you to deliver your presentation. Alas, you can't store up oxygen from your morning jog or your brisk walk before you go on. You've got to keep it flowing if you, your body and your brain are going to give a successful performance.

When your nerves get the better of you, your breathing becomes shallow, that is, restricted to the top of your lungs. This kind of breathing is exhausting, forces you to gasp when you speak and causes the pitch of your voice to rise an octave into a shrill, high pitch – something no man wants. Here's what to do:

- Start by centring your body. If standing, balance yourself evenly on both feet. When you do this, you align your body and allow your vocal chords to work in harmony with your diaphragm and lungs.

- Breathe deeply and slowly. Aim to fill the bottom of your lungs first, so your tummy expands. To enable the full use of your powerful and all-important diaphragmatic muscles don't wear a tight belt. Let the air rise from the lower to the middle, then upper part of the lungs. You want to feel the air enter your chest almost as if it is blowing up through your throat to your voice.

Take regular, relaxed breaths as you speak. Always breathe in and wait to begin speaking until you **are** exhaling. Your voice will be deeper and sound more controlled. Speaking at the beginning of the exhale, or even at the top of the inhale, makes you sound desperate and causes you to gasp. This is particularly important when you are being questioned. Waiting for the exhale means there will be a natural pause, for a fleeting few seconds. But the sound that comes out is well worth waiting for, more confident and assured.

Lubricate Your Vocal Chords

Avoid hot stimulants such as tea or coffee, especially with milk, prior to speaking. Other drinks that don't help are fizzy or very cold ones. It's best to lubricate your voice with warm water containing a slice of lemon, or just drink plain still water (at room temperature).

If your voice dries up while you are speaking and no water is available, pause for a moment on the pretext of referring to visual aid or your notes, whatever, and chew on your tongue for a few seconds. This will get the saliva going and help to lubricate your throat. But that's a measure to resort to in desperation. You are in charge of the success of your presentation, so should never go on without first checking that water is readily to hand.

Consult the Experts

If after going through some of these exercises you still feel that your voice is detrimental to your image, consult a good speech therapist. A trained voice coach, speech pathologist, even drama coach can assess your problems and recommend specific remedies. Remember that your voice is worth 38 per cent of the impact you make, so don't allow yours to lessen your impact.

CHAPTER 12

YOUR IMAGE ACROSS THE TABLE

MEETINGS are a regular opportunity to present yourself and show your worth to superiors and peers in business. Although probably half of the meetings you attend are almost a complete waste of time, it is at meetings that most business eventually gets conducted. Whether you are a participant or the chair-person, how you perform is critical to your career advancement.

Many careers have been made simply by how someone handled a meeting. When I was Director of Operations for a Presidential Task Force on Refugee Resettlement, I remember being so impressed by how a young Vietnamese spoke and comported himself in a meeting that I hired him. His courage and clarity of communication, even with limited English, and while flanked by pompous bureaucrats and clever lobbyists, showed me a talent the government needed. He proved me right and went on to enjoy a brilliant career in the federal government and later still became a highly successful entrepreneur.

A meeting is basically any discussion that occurs between two or more people, but this can take many forms. Think of all the different types and settings for the meetings you attend in your normal business week: Breakfast meetings, One-to-one interviews, Staff meetings, Sales meetings, Team meetings, Negotiations, Board meetings, Lunch meetings, Conferences, Business/social meetings, Professional club meetings, Public meetings, Training sessions, Brainstorming sessions.

In meetings you reveal a lot about yourself and your potential. You show whether you have leadership skills, interpersonal skills, communication skills, presentation skills, are on top of your job, can be trusted and relied upon.

Reflect on the regular meetings you attend. Who among your colleagues is always very effective? Does he or she approach every meeting in the same way? If so, what can you learn from this? Evaluate the strengths of each of your peers and rank them on a scale of one to ten in terms of effectiveness in handling themselves at meetings. Undoubtedly you have formed definite opinions about each of them. So too have they of you. How do you think they would rank your abilities in meetings on the same one to ten scale.

GROUP MEETINGS

As a Participant

When you get invited to a meeting, you are called as part of a group for a purpose. If that purpose isn't clear you should find out the objectives of the chair-person, to help you prepare. When a group is called to discuss one or several issues that implicitly means that one individual doesn't have the responsibility for sorting things out. You must do it as a group, for the benefit of the organisation; the responsibility is shared. You are all individuals contributing different expertise but in the end must agree on collective solutions.

How you perform at meetings is critical to your career advancement

Too often we forget that we must share responsibility, and we go to meetings with our own agendas which may be counter to that of the group. When you isolate yourself in this way, and play to win or score on points only important to yourself, you become resented and might eventually be excluded from meetings. You might think 'great, they are such a waste of time'. But if you thus lose or relinquish your position at the centre of policy and decision-making, you will become vulnerable.

Never expect to succeed in a meeting 'on a wing and a prayer'. Preparation is essential to your performance. Even if you won't necessarily be called upon to present, swot up on as many issues as possible so that you can contribute. Whenever possible, and without overdoing it, always try to state your views, or ask an intelligent question. Sometimes the chair is very rigid and controls participation but for normal staff meetings, brainstorming sessions, etc. which make up most of your meetings, try to be actively involved.

Here are some guidelines for handling yourself in meetings with subordinates, peers, and supervisors.

With Subordinates

- Be supportive and encouraging. Supply everyone with an agenda in advance or, if called at short notice, let them know the purpose of the meeting so that they can organise their thoughts and papers in readiness.

- Resist the temptation to finish their sentences or criticise anyone on a personal level, although the temptation to do so may be great. If you shoot down one the rest will clam up and you'll get nowhere.

- Have someone take minutes or at least note decisions taken and the action points requiring follow-up. Send the minutes out within 24 hours of the meeting, noting in them exactly who is responsible for following up what.

- If the purpose of the meeting was to move a project forward or to get things done, establish a timetable or a date for the next meeting so everyone knows what is expected of them.

- When it comes to your image, be sure not to overwhelm. Wear user-friendly colours – the midtone suit, fun tie – rather than your more severe, high-powered look. Research shows that people open up, feel freer to speak their minds if you wear non-threatening shades. But don't go so far as to dress down and lose authority. Always begin the meeting with your jacket on and take it off only if you feel you need to break down barriers and create more informality so that the staff feel more welcome to speak their minds.

With Peers

- Your aim should be seen as collegial but also to earn authority as a leader among equals. Your boss will eventually want to be informed about what the group is thinking. So, offer to write up the minutes and submit them on behalf of the group.

- If an issue on the agenda is yours and central to your interests, don't leave it until the meeting to win agreement. Lobby key people ahead of time as to the merits of your idea. Be seen as open to discuss the potential weakness of your proposal; answer as objectively as possible. Even if you are feeling emotional about an objection, don't show it. Your detractors will seize upon your weakness if they sense it or, worse still, feel sorry for you.

- Keep summarising the benefits of your views and why your proposal meets the objectives set.

- It will be very important to be sensitive to your image when dressing for such a meeting. If it is a brainstorming session and you look turned-out for a board presentation; you will immediately create barriers. You want to have authority but you need to be persuasive in gaining it. Look authoritative – wear a strong suit – but soften the look with a pastel shirt and not a terribly severe tie.

With Supervisors

- Simply put, you are there to help them. Your aim is to be resourceful, to be seen as collaborating in the objectives.

- In these meetings with senior executives, you have an opportunity to shine as well as to be supportive. The 'yes man' makes life easy for the chair but wins no reputation as an individual to be given more responsibility.

- The 'prophet of doom' who never has a good or constructive contribution is also tiresome. If you have reservations or disagree, say so, but avoid getting a reputation as someone who always shoots ideas down. Leaders are positive not negative people.

- In meetings with supervisors you need to show respect. Save your hysterical ties for anywhere but here. The more important the meeting the more sober your clothes should be, with the most serious sessions demanding your darkest suit, a white shirt and most elegant but restrained tie.

- Show the bearing of a man in charge and one who can be relied upon. Organise yourself before you arrive. Collate your papers into order and bring them into the meeting assembled in a nice leather file. Always have a note pad and take efficient notes, especially when the boss sums up or determines an Action Point. Use a good fountain pen with a fresh cartridge.

Other Roles

There are many other roles that people assume at meetings:

- There is the **Disrupter** who always arrives late or is constantly dashing in and out for messages. This person is just saying that he considers himself to be superior to the group and that it doesn't merit his attention.

- The **Evaluator** can lend a significant contribution in weighing pros and cons, but should avoid always filling this role and occasionally have a personally decisive view on things.

- The **Nonentity** remains part of the furniture, which may be undemanding but will mean his days as a player are numbered. If you don't/can't participate, you are taking up valuable space and will lose your chance to become more involved. More involvement brings more responsibility. More responsibility means more visibility, which means advancement.

As the Chair

To succeed in this role at a meeting takes more skill than simply knowing technically how to do it. A well run meeting takes preparation plus people, communication and management skills.

- In preparation, always develop a focused agenda. Limit it to one page, preferably no more than a dozen lines in length. Assign presentations ahead of time, getting your key people to lead discussions. Your role is to get the facts out, generate discussion that leads to proposed solutions, evaluate the pros and cons of the solutions and gain agreement on the best one.

- The most effective way to move an agenda is to limit the number of participants. Only involve people who are essential and can make a contribution. If the issues require deliberation by a greater number of people, have your managers go through the same exercise with their teams and present the concerns and recommendations of their staff.

- Let participants know what will be expected of them. If you want their input, back up, research on anything, give them ample notice. If you don't, you have only yourself to blame if the meeting degenerates into an unruly and unproductive session of off-the-cuff opinions.

- Encourage individual presentations but take issue only with the ideas and analyses, not the people themselves.

- Meet in the morning whenever possible, when people are most alert. If the agenda will take all day allow frequent breaks. Better to start very early and allow a real break, say one-and-a-half hours, at lunch-time for people to refresh themselves. Encourage a few ten minute recesses and suggest that people take a walk outside where the oxygen might be fresher and help increase the blood supply to their brains.

- Choose a meeting room that will be conducive to discussion. One that is too small becomes very claustrophobic in no time, one that is too large and cavernous creates a more formal atmosphere that inhibits discussion. One that has a noisy location will constantly be disturbed.

How to Dress

Even the most informal brainstorming meeting is a battle ground for status and recognition. To maintain yours or win attention, dress as formally as your normal work environment allows. Obviously, if yours is usually a sports jacket and trousers operation to show up in a pin-stripe suit would be inappropriate. Your colleagues would immediately suspect you of being on some power trip. In this situation, wear your best sports jacket and a tie, and don't take your jacket off during the meeting (even though many of your colleagues, no doubt, will do). Wearing a jacket throughout a meeting will give you more authority, without overstating the point.

If presenting, wear your darkest suit, a plain shirt and a strong but not distracting tie. Keep your jacket buttoned while standing. Your hands will be much on display, so be sure your nails are clean (and preferably manicured). Use a good fountain pen (remembering to load beforehand with a fresh cartridge).

Where to Sit

When you arrive at a meeting without assigned seating it can be a nightmare figuring out where to sit to achieve your objectives. In some meetings you know you are in for a confrontation with an adversary; in others you need to present and be seen by the greatest number. In some meetings you simply want to disappear.

Here are some general guidelines on how to sit yourself strategically:

- If you want recognition always sit within good eye contact of the decision-makers (who may not always include the chair).

- If presenting, arrive early and select your best vantage point. At a long table you are best in the middle of one side; at an oval table at one of the narrow ends.

- To mitigate a confrontation, sit next to the person ready to chew you out. It is far more difficult to attack from the side. At all costs, avoid sitting directly opposite that person.

- To avoid recognition, sit in a 'blind spot' for the chair, your supervisor or the key participant; that is, where it is physically difficult to see you – if such a position is available; if it isn't a large meeting, probably not.

- If you are a junior or new participant, wait to be told where to sit.

Positive Body Language

The BBC once asked me to analyse the dynamics of a corporate staff meeting by watching a video of the proceedings, with the volume turned off. They wanted me to explain to viewers the body signals that the participants were using and how easy and accurate it is to interpret personalities, attitudes and relationships without hearing a word that was spoken. It was quite obvious who respected whom, who was written off by everyone and who was antagonistic against whom. Do you realise how much you expose of your true feelings for colleagues through your behaviour at meetings?

You may be able to control your behaviour in short meetings but longer ones test everyone's patience and inevitably, through fatigue, we begin to send messages loud and clear without opening our mouths.

You can use your behaviour to impress others or to undermine yourself during meetings. The box on page 130 tells you how.

ONE-TO-ONE: JOB INTERVIEWS

Perhaps the best example of the one-to-one meeting and one most crucial to everyone's career is the Job Interview. As we at CMB often get asked to advise people on what to wear and how to handle themselves in an interview, it merits special discussion here.

The first thing to realise is that the best qualified don't always get the jobs. No, they go rather to the people most skilled at convincing others that they are right for the vacancy in question. Even if you don't have all the necessary qualifications and experience, if you want the job and know you can do it, you should be able to sell yourself. You have lots of intangible assets that every employer wants: like being organised, hard-working, able to deal with

---

WATCH YOUR BODY LANGUAGE

Impressive Signals	Undermining Signals
Sitting upright and alert. Sit forward to convey real interest	Slouching in your chair
Keep your eyes on the speaker	Look down at notes, out of the window, at the ceiling
Take notes, not constantly, but key points	Doodle
Turn your body to the speaker/chair	Physically turn away
When listening keep your body 'open': arms leaning-forward on table; relaxed to sides of your body; hands gently folded	Fold your arms tightly across your body (says, 'I'm not listening')
Use open gestures: hands open or up as if serving an idea to your colleagues	Use closed, threatening gestures like the preaching forefinger to make your points
Smile and use humour to alleviate tension whenever appropriate	Deadpan, growling, or cynical expressions

---

difficult people; and these can more than compensate for being a bit short on credentials. And above all you can exude enthusiasm. Studies show that 90 per cent of Personnel Directors consider enthusiasm a vital qualification for any job.

How to Dress

In the first three minutes, the interviewer will decide if s/he *isn't* going to hire you. You should be able to see that the whole exercise is perfunctory after three or four minutes simply by their behaviour.

If you pass the three-minute hurdle and still note interest, they haven't decided to hire you necessarily but you do have a chance. That is why your appearance is vital to jumping over that initial hurdle with confidence.

In a survey of top recruiters and personnel directors, we at CMB learned that the key factors that create a favourable impression (in order of judged importance) at an interview are:

1. Wearing a smart suit
2. Being well-groomed
3. Looking fit and healthy
4. Carrying a smart attaché or brief-case.

To help you create a positive first impression here's some advice on what to wear to an interview.

- Wear the best suit you can afford or borrow, and make sure it is pressed.
- Choose neutral rather than loud colours but show more flair if applying to a creative industry.
- Look current but never trendy (unless applying for a position in fashion).
- Avoid flashy ties, and accessories.
- Don't wear any aftershave.
- Aim for understated elegance.
- Be sure your shoes are well-polished – lace-ups not slip-on shoes.
- Use a neat, small note pad and fountain pen to take notes.
- Go for a brisk walk before the interview to look healthy.
- Cover any spots, using a medicated coverstick.
- Have clean hair. Don't wear a greasy gel, the wet-look or an outlandish style.
- If you sport shoulder-length hair, tie it back. Better still, if you really want the job, get your hair cut short. Prejudice against men with long hair is still prevalent.
- Be clean-shaven (you can grow your beard back after you get the job).
- Have clean, manicured nails which will be on view as you take notes.
- Leave your coat in reception.
- Keep jewellery to a minimum.

How to Behave

What you say in an interview is important but how you speak and your general behaviour are under far more scrutiny. In addition to finding out if you can actually do the job, the interviewer is probing to see how you will fit into the corporate culture.

- Be enthusiastic without going overboard.

- If scared stiff don't allow your body to betray you. Run around the block before the interview to release the pent-up adrenalin. But allow time to get your breath back.

- Shake hands upon meeting the interviewer and look him/her straight in the eye with a smile. Shake hands on leaving.

- Show excellent manners. Say 'please' and 'thank you', for example, if a receptionist brings you a coffee. Don't scratch yourself or nervously pick at your cuticles, or worse.

- Sit relaxed in the chair but don't slump. Don't sit too far forward unless in a very soft chair/sofa.

- Don't become too relaxed, even if you think things are going well. Think 'professional'.

- Don't joke around, aside from the odd pleasantry or witticism. No one wants a clown, unless that's the job you are applying for.

- Take out a pen and note pad at the beginning of the interview and jot down a few notes throughout. Shows interest and attention to details.

- If the interviewer takes a phone call that is running on, after a few minutes take out an article from your attaché or brief-case and begin reading it. This reading helps you look intelligent, shows you don't like to waste time, and allows the interviewer to conduct the telephone call without feeling under scrutiny.

Likely Questions

The job interview is like a sales call but you are the only product you've got. Don't expect one act to go down the same with all interviewers. They are all different. You need to have sharp, honest, positive replies to all the standard questions. Here are some examples, but no doubt you've met with many others.

'Why are you interested in this job?'

'Why are you leaving your present job?'

'Why were you made redundant?'

'What experience are you most proud of in your career thus far?'

'What are your strengths? Weaknesses?'

'You have different (or no) experience. How can you do the job?'

'Why should we hire you?'

'What are your interests?'

Answers to these and similar questions you need to have prepared. But never jump to answer the questions. Take your time; answer only as you are exhaling.

Size up the interviewer: what response did s/he seem to like best and why? Some people like examples of your experiences explained; others want to see examples of what you did. Some want you to be brief, others like you to elaborate. *Listen* and *observe* the interviewer so that you can pick up the signals and give him/her what they like, how they like it.

Use a few non-important interviews as trial runs for the vital ones. You'll learn through practice and discover how to project yourself in your best light. For those who seem most polished at interviewing are former students of the art who have studied, practised and succeeded. You can succeed too if you make the same effort.

YOUR HANDSHAKE TELLS ALL

Do you know the impression your handshake leaves on others? We have all experienced bad handshakes and know how they interfere with communication. When another man gives you a real bone-crushing squeeze you immediately suspect he is on a power trip. A limp-wristed, wet-fish handshake leaves most of us cold. How you shake hands with potential customers and clients, whether male or female, says everything about your confidence, professionalism, and urbanity.

The bone-crusher impresses no-one

Give people the space they need

The Bone-Crusher

Men sometimes try to score points when shaking hands by grinding the other's hand to pulp. Avoid doing this, and also remember that an over-bearing grip that may be acceptable to men can actually hurt women. Our hands can ache for several minutes after such an encounter, which does little to enhance our first impression of you.

Keep your distance

We all have a comfort zone, i.e. the amount of space we need to have around ourselves to feel comfortable. It is the distance we like to keep between our-selves and other people. When meeting someone for the first time, play it safe by keeping a decent distance from their body (don't get any closer than 70cm or a little over 2 feet). Also, watch to see how quickly they move away or if they stay close after you have shaken hands. Follow their body language by lingering if they do or providing more space if you feel they need it.

Men often take liberties, wittingly or unwittingly, when being introduced to a woman. You do not endear yourself nor score points by encroaching on a woman's comfort zone, especially if you take the added liberty of grabbing her with both hands (above right). Even when meeting a female business associate who you have known for some time, unless on really friendly terms (agreeable to both of you), you are advised to treat her respectfully by giving her enough space along with a professional, pleasant handshake.

A welcome greeting

A Good Shake

The best handshake is one that is direct, firm and friendly (above). It is direct when your arm extends straight in front of you, rather than across the body or away from your body. A firm handshake means that your hands meet 'web to web' (i.e. the 'web' between your thumb and forefinger connects with that of the other person's hand) and that you exert a bit of pressure to their hand once or twice. A friendly handshake is always greeted with a smile and a courteous salutation like 'Nice to meet you' or 'Good to see you again'.

Who's first?

Salesmen who cold-call are advised not to extend their hands first to a potential customer as it is more likely to get a negative response as the person's time and space is being encroached by someone unknown and uninvited. But in a normal business circumstances, e.g. when you arrive for a meeting outside the office, you should extend your hand in a forthright, friendly manner. If you are the junior in a group of more senior people don't take the initiative with handshakes. Let the top person start the introductions and follow suit as naturally as possible.

CHAPTER 13

PRESENTING YOURSELF

SOONER or later you'll be given the opportunity, or landed with the terrifying prospect – depending on your viewpoint – of speaking to an audience. All successful people know that their career progression, to a significant extent, is based upon their exposure (opportunities to be seen and heard) both within their own organisation and outside among clients and peers. To turn down opportunities of gaining visibility is to shoot yourself in the career foot. So, if you find the prospect of public speaking daunting, take heart from the fact that most people are more frightened of speaking to an audience than of death itself, and take yourself firmly in hand.

I am going to assume that you are the type to take up the gauntlet when offered to speak. You have already had the benefit of reading Chapter Eleven – The Image of Your Voice – but if still in doubt about your ability, or if interested in improving your technique, do consider investing in a good training course as such an experience will greatly advance your prospects. The objective of public speaking training is not simply to learn how to prepare and deliver a talk but also how to enjoy the experience and to be yourself.

Although technically you may be giving a presentation, remember that what you are doing also is **presenting yourself**. Within the first three minutes or so of speaking, your audience will decide whether or not they'll bother to listen. That is why so many books and training programmes on presentation skills stress the importance of a good opening. But along with arresting the audience's interest in the first minute with what you say, you want to grab them with your image.

Depending on the size of the presentation or on whether or not you are appearing on TV (or video), you will require different advice. So let me set the stage for some key presentation situations that you might encounter and give you guidelines that can be adapted to similar situations.

THE INTERNAL MEETING (up to 15 people)

A small business presentation might be a formal one, such as a board meeting, or a less formal one, such as a training session. The two key questions to ask are:

1. **What is the purpose of the presentation?**
   - Are you there merely to inform and not to invite much participation?
   - Or are you there to present ideas for discussion?

2. **Who is the audience?**
   - Internal colleagues?
   - Peers, subordinates or supervisors?
   - Clients or potential customers?
   - Industry peers?
   - The press or general public?

THE FORMAL PRESENTATION

When your purpose is primarily to inform your audience and not to elicit discussion you want to project your authority in your dress and confidence in your behaviour. Here are some tips to consider.

What to Wear

To convey authority in what you are presenting, dress your most conservative. Select your darkest suit, mindful of how dark you can go without looking as if the suit is wearing you. Your best shirt would be your white one (either pure white or ivory). Pastels – almost white and showing just a hint of colour – are also good. Avoid stripes, as they will distract your audience and force them to look away intermittently to relieve their eyes.

Your tie should be interesting, neither too safe nor too flamboyant. The goal is for you to be seen, listened to and for the information to be believed. If your image is *insignificant*, as if you just popped in without preparation, then what you are saying won't be convincing. The power of your words needs to correlate with the power of your image.

Always keep your jacket buttoned when speaking. Unload your pockets so that they lie flat. If your jacket doesn't fall nicely when buttoned, don't wear that suit for an important presentation.

Your Body Language

You want your information to be accepted, so your gestures, behaviour and voice need to be as convincing as the words you use. Avoid defensive postures like 'hugging yourself' or clasping your hands behind your back. Worse still are closed gestures like crossing your arms in front of you which only conveys your defensiveness and concern about what you are saying.

To present the information and yourself in the best light keep your body *open*. If using notes, keep one hand at your side, or use natural hand movements with your palms up. As keen as you are to be believed, don't let your gestures *preach*, that is, use a pointing finger for emphasis or, if seated at a table, fold your hands and make a steeple with your fingers (which conveys arrogance).

Open gestures make your statements more acceptable

Regardless of how serious the subject may be, the occasional smile (not grin) will help you win acceptance. Use eye contact with everyone in the room, regularly and deliberately, as if you are speaking directly to that person – even if it is only for a fleeting second or two. Don't avoid eye contact with any detractors. Taking them head on will show you are confident and even stifle some challenges.

Make sure your voice is convincing. End all your declarations in a low, measured tone, as if what you have said is a statement of fact.

THE INFORMAL PRESENTATION

In a more relaxed environment, or in one where you genuinely want people to open up and participate, less authority in dress and behaviour is required and more personality and selfless consideration of others' opinions is in order. A training seminar, staff meeting or brainstorming session would be examples. For these presentations you want to appear open, welcoming. Here's what to consider in these situations.

What to Wear

Select more user-friendly colours. You want the attention to be on your face, so draw everyone's eye contact to yours by wearing a mid-tone suit, say, a medium charcoal, mid-blue, greyed-green or slate. Pastel shirts are friendlier than sober white so try a blue, lilac or pink one. Your tie can be fun but not ridiculous. Remember you are still making a presentation, so you don't want your tie or anything else to distract from your face.

Depending on the situation, a sports jacket and trousers might be a preferable option to a more high-powered suit. You still need to be in charge, so a jacket is essential armour to maintain control, even as a facilitator. Never, ever, think that going without a jacket and tie will be acceptable. Your audience might love the informality but you won't be half as believable as you would be if dressed more appropriately.

Many trainers, in particular, have been lured into thinking that a relaxed dress code at training courses helps the participants relax. What, in fact, happens is that you add stress when they are there on business without their usual 'suit of armour'. Trousers, jeans and sports shirts are only advised for weekend seminars on a non-business subject away from the usual work environment.

Your Body Language

You need to employ a completely different tone in your gestures, behaviour and voice to encourage others during an informal presentation. Your questions will be open to elicit discussion; so, too, should your gestures be. Don't stand rigid, glued to one spot at the head of a table. Best to move around, extend your hand to invite someone in particular to speak. Lightly touch people on the shoulder or arm when appropriate. Sit down from time to time when others are speaking, so that you become part of the listening group.

Be an active listener when others are speaking – keep your eyes on them as if what they are saying is very compelling, even if it is not. Reinforce the right of others to express an opinion, and take notes, reiterating the key points that participants are making. Nod your head when you agree with speakers. When you don't, just take it on board and try not to show it; allow others an opportunity to rebut contrary viewpoints from time to time rather than always being the one having to defend or take issue. If you take a too rigid control of the meeting, other people will be discouraged from speaking

Win support by being an
active listener as well
as speaker

– and you could lose an excellent idea without ever even knowing. The ability to run an informal meeting is essential to building your reputation and rapport among your colleagues, subordinates and managers. Develop a style that makes everyone feel good about participating while still maintaining distinction as the man at the helm.

LARGE AUDIENCE PRESENTATIONS

Speaking to a group of more that 15 or so people becomes a performance. In addition to being a capable and talented professional, you must now move into the area of entertainment. Don't be alarmed, I am not recommending tedious jokes or song and dance routines as the means to enliven a presentation. No, rather you can grab your audience's attention – and hold it – by polishing both your speech and your image. When a great package holds a terrific product you've got the winning combination.

You are the Key Prop

Students of presentation skills learn that a good presentation to a large audience is never just verbal – it always requires good visual aids, too. Any audience today, like yourself, expects images to help convey the messages. On average, your audience sees two hours of television a day, is bombarded with slick commercial radio advertising while driving to work, reads newspapers and business material deliberately presented in a style that is visually attractive and accessible, and has probably taken a presentation course that stressed the importance of visual aids. Props are needed to enliven a large presentation, as well as to help organise and emphasise your message. But always remember that your Number One Prop is **yourself**.

For a large audience presentation you need to think theatre. You need to project your voice, preferably electronically with a microphone, and to enlarge your every gesture to correlate with the size of your audience. Just as important, you need to draw attention to yourself and help hold the audience's gaze by means of your appearance.

One rarely succeeds in doing a large presentation without a lot of homework. I am not referring to your speech here, but to the logistics of the presentation. Without knowing these – the room layout, staging, background, lighting, etc., your appearance may fail completely.

Room Layout

It's essential to study the layout of the room, to discern how visible you will be to the audience. If speaking from the floor, that is at the same level as your audience, be sure you are tall enough to be seen.

I'm only 5 feet 3 inches, and regularly insist on a platform to speak from so the audience can see every bit of me. If they can't see you clearly, you will become merely a talking head, which is hardly enough visual animation to keep your audience's undivided attention. Just think for a moment how easy it is to let your attention wander if, say, you are in a theatre, cinema or sports crowd and your view is impeded. It is also intensely frustrating. Once I didn't have the opportunity to see the location for a presentation, when I was an after-dinner speaker at a beautiful castle in Salzburg. I had been training all day in modern facilities but that night I was to be speaking somewhere 'special'. Whenever an organiser tells me that I get very nervous.

The dining room was packed and the head table, where I was seated, was in front – and under poor light. Flanked by people who towered over me, whose own presentations went off fine, I knew I was doomed when it came to my turn to speak. Just as I was being introduced I noticed a central staircase leading to the dining room. I indicated that I would like to speak from the stairs, asked everyone if they would please adjust their seats as necessary, and spoke from there. Despite having the after dinner 'graveyard slot', I thus succeeded in grabbing their attention and holding it. But try to avoid such desperate last minute manoeuvres by seeing the set-up beforehand, whenever possible.

Staging

At formal conferences you can expect to be on stage either seated at a table or introduced and left at a lectern from which you deliver your speech. If you are seen seated on a stage, with or without a table, be sure that your clothes don't let you down.

Your trousers must be long enough and your socks high enough so that when you cross your legs your audience doesn't see a flash of shins – hairy or otherwise. Be sure your shoes are beautifully polished and in tip-top condition.

At the podium or lectern make sure that your entire face, at least, is seen. Ideally, you should be more visible, say, down to your chest area, to hold your audience's attention.

Formal, prepared speeches read at a lectern usually put audiences to sleep, unless under 10 minutes in duration. If you don't have the time to commit your talk to memory, can't 'wing-it' with cue-cards or an outline, or find an autocue nerve-racking, then you will need to break the presentation up at points which allow you to move slightly away from the lectern (assuming the microphone can still pick you up) and speak seemingly extemporaneously. Aim to be seen in full, once or twice, to break the monotony of the talking head image.

Try making your introduction away from the lectern, in a more natural way, to impress the audience with your confidence and let them get a good look at you. Then retreat to the lectern to give your speech. Near the end, come forward and present yourself again to the audience with a closing remark.

Background

To ensure that you stand out and are seen in a large platform presentation, it is essential to find out the colour of the backdrop. Often this will consist of very dark curtains, and if you stand in front of them in a dark suit you will simply disappear. Instead, dress in complementary contrast to your backdrop.

Lighting

It might seem an obvious point, that you need an efficient spotlight on you in order to be seen, but how often have you noticed someone speaking in almost total darkness, particularly when delivering a slide presentation. Those little lectern lights which help you read your notes aren't enough. You need to be well-lit the entire time, if you are to hold your audience's attention.

Lighting comes in a variety of blue and yellow tones. If speaking somewhere other than in a modern business conference facility, check out what kind of lights they use. If the lights are very blue and you are in a navy suit and blue shirt you'll fade away. If the lighting is extreme, either very blue or very yellow, be sure you choose your suit and shirt to provide sufficient contrast with the lights. Staging technicians are often very helpful. Better still, bring a colleague along to advise on how you look under these particular lights.

What to Wear

Remember that in contrast to a small presentation, the large audience is theatre. Hence, you need to think of the impact of your 'costume' on the audience.

Go for contrasting colours, an impeccably fitted suit and spotless grooming. A medium to dark suit, white shirt (or ivory if best for your facial colouring) and an elegant but strong tie is best. The pattern of the tie should not distract from your face, but shouldn't be a solid colour, unless the tie is an elegant woven silk one that picks up some light. Use a subtle silk pocket handkerchief to break-up the solid expanse of suit. Team in the colours with the tie but use a different, indistinguishable pattern or solid colour.

Other tips on presenting yourself successfully:

- Empty all your pockets so that your suit lies flat and there are no unseemly bulges.

- Button-up your jacket, otherwise the focus will be on your midriff, perhaps not your most flattering point.

- Avoid loud colours and patterns in shirts and ties.

- Lightly spray unruly hair into place beforehand.

- Avoid wearing glasses if possible. If you do need them to see your notes be sure your eyes are seen at the centre of the lenses (no half glasses). If you need to present regularly, consider getting a non-reflective coating on your lenses to minimise the glare of spotlights which, otherwise, may be all the audience will see.

- Your shirt collars should be flawlessly pressed and lie flat under your jacket. The half-Windsor knot is the most elegant (see Chapter Seven).

- Lightly powder your face with translucent powder to prevent shining. If you have a receding or non-existent hairline dust your pate as well, to maintain contact with your eyes not the top of your head. Remember, such tricks are NOT the exclusive prerogative of women.

- If you have dark circles around your eyes, use a concealer stick to lighten up this area. Otherwise, from a distance you will look unwell – perhaps even ghoulish! Smear a little of the concealer on to the tip of your index finger, then tap this gently all over the under-eye area, making sure that it is evenly dispersed. If you're too heavy-handed with this, you will soon have bags under your eyes as well as shadows.

CHAPTER 14

IN THE PUBLIC EYE

THE more resourceful and successful you are in your career, the more likely it is that sooner or later you will be asked to speak on behalf of your organisation, to represent it under the scrutiny of the media. The first opportunity produces a 'fight or flight' response in most people, particularly the untrained. Even the most capable, articulate manager can appear incompetent if unprepared for an encounter with an inquisitive journalist. Hence, it is wise to think through how best to handle being in the Public Eye, especially if you ever consider choosing a Public life, such as becoming a politician.

TELEVISION

Handling the media, particularly television, takes a set of skills that most of us have to learn. Few can 'wing' an interview with no training or preparation and hope to come off well. We have all witnessed punters make fools of themselves on television. You know, the local news report where an unsuspecting company spokes-person was sent into the studio ill-prepared and poorly-groomed for a tough interview. It is embarrassing to watch when a no doubt normally articulate and nice person comes over either as a crook or an idiot.

TV is an art-form and, to succeed, you need to learn the rules of the game in order to present yourself and your case successfully. You would never give an important presentation or chair a meeting without giving considerable forethought to your objectives and how you want to come across, as well as what you will wear. Television requires equal, if not more, planning and preparation because the stakes are so high.

PREPARING FOR A TV INTERVIEW

You must do your homework thoroughly before any TV interview; just knowing you are wanted on a breakfast show to discuss a particular issue about which you feel reasonably well informed isn't enough.

Research the following:

- What kind of programme will you be on? There's a world of difference between hard news and a chat show. Sometimes they will discuss the same issues but the treatment is light years apart.

- How much time do you have for your interview? The researcher should tell you this quite precisely. For example, you might be part of a 5 minute piece but only likely to be asked one or two questions and get only a minute of airtime. Prepare to make it count.

- Who else will be appearing with you? Expect the format to include a protagonist (possibly yourself) and an antagonist (possibly a competitor, disgruntled employee, irate customer, union official, consumer activist, politician, etc.). If no one else is participating in the interview, expect your interviewer to be the 'devil's advocate'.

- Who is the interviewer? You might be familiar with the programme but interviewers work on a rota, so you may not get the one you hope for. Once known, watch him/her beforehand or ask the researcher for tapes of their interviews to get a sense of their style and interview technique. Don't be diffident about asking; it's a reasonable request and tapes *are* available.

- Where will the interview be held? An in-studio appearance requires different preparation from one on location, for example, at your office. If the latter, never agree to begin filming until you have checked exactly where you will be positioned. Ask to see the monitor before you begin and eliminate anything distracting or likely to be misinterpreted.

HANDLING THE INTERVIEW

If asked to be interviewed on television, make sure you have your own objectives very clear. You will be hit with all sorts of questions, some irrelevant to the central message you need and want to convey. Your main worry should never be the interviewer but the clock. Time is always of the essence. So your message must be concise, effective and premeditated.

Your Message

Accepting that time is short, focus your message on a few key points, kept simple but reinforced by everything you say.

If you are brought in to defend a charge, whether or not fairly levied, prepare ahead of time how you will respond. Write out your reply and practise it on others before the interview. Be positive, own up if relevant and necessary, present remedies and, above all, be pleasant. Even if you have been boxed into a tight corner and you are on the defensive, try not to look or sound as if you are.

In some situations, an interview can be vital to business, if not a turning point one way or another in your career. If in doubt about your ability to tackle tough questions and defend your position, have colleagues rehearse you on likely questions ahead of time, so you get your message flowing smoothly.

The Interviewer

Believe it or not, s/he is human, too. Many first-time interviewees are terrified by their potential interviewer. Just remember, they have the edge over you in being familiar with the technology and the set, and they know what the questions will be, but you have the edge with your expertise – which they need. A good researcher will have provided them with a brief on your subject but they still have to think on their feet. So, never project signals that convey you feel inferior to the interviewer. Sure, s/he is no doubt highly intelligent and skilled in the art of interviewing, but s/he isn't the specialist that you are in your field. Treat the interviewer neither as a superior nor an inferior, but as your professional equal.

However much you may be provoked, keep your composure and never attack back. The interviewer is familiar to the audience. You are the outsider who can readily become the *bad guy* if you show any hostility. Keep your answer sharp, to the point. If you have to dig, do so with a smile – not a smirk – to take the sting out of a tough reply. Your goal is to appear relaxed, open, competent and trustworthy.

YOUR TV IMAGE

If you expect an increasing role in television, it is wise to get some professional coaching ahead of time. It is essential for you to see how you come across under questioning as well as to see how you look in terms of style. Mock TV interviews on video are illuminating, not soul destroying. They give most people greater confidence in handling the real thing.

If short notice makes it impossible for you to receive coaching before an important television interview, here are some general guidelines to help you handle your first appearance on the small screen with success.

What to Wear

Forget about all the wonderful shirts and ties in your wardrobe and learn what is most effective on camera. We've all watched presenters or their guests who have projected a distracting image on screen. You can't recall a thing they said but will remember their tie or weird hairstyle.'

Certain colours are enhancing on camera and others are not. Avoid extremes, such as very light or very dark colours. Black or dark navy are overwhelming on camera. So, wear a suit that is medium in tone, with negligible or no pattern. The medium blues, soft charcoals, greyed browns and greens are especially effective. Use the latter tones (soft browns, greens) only for a light-hearted, weekend or magazine format. If acting as the company spokes-person, play it safe in traditional business blue or grey.

White shirts bleach out on screen, making all caucasians look pale and uninteresting. Opt instead for light pastels such as a light yellow, pink, blue or lilac. The colour should be almost indistinguishable but will have the effect of making you look healthy. If you have a heavy beardline, wear a pink shirt rather than a blue or lilac one, which can cast a shadow, making the beard look much heavier, even after a wet shave. Solid or plain shirts are recommended in preference to stripes, which are just too distracting; they 'dance', that is, strobe on camera.

When selecting a suitable tie, remember that strong pinks, such as magenta through to red, defy clear focusing in most studios, under most conditions, and have an effect known as 'bleeding', that is, where the outlines get fuzzy and seem to run, like a dye. The more sophisticated the set the better capable it is to handle strong colours, but assume that your local news station or satellite studio is ill-equipped and needs other colours for best effect – blues, greens, purples or turquoise shades. Choose an elegant, muted pattern in a matt-finished silk (that is, without any shine). Moiré silks are inadvisable, as the woven texture combined with the shine of the silk can strobe.

Make-up for Television

Both women and men require make-up for television, in order to look polished and well-groomed. Most male presenters use sunbeds regularly or wear a skin foundation deeper than their normal skin tone in order to look healthy.

Make-up is a must for everyone appearing in front of the camera

Never leave your arrival at the studios so late that you don't have time to visit the make-up artist. And never agree to go on camera without being professionally made up, unless you know from long experience exactly how to prepare yourself.

Make-up artists are highly skilled at making you look your best. Here are the factors that normally need attention:

High Colouring　If you have a ruddy skin tone, burst capillaries or redness you need to be 'toned-down' with a light application of green or mint adjuster, to balance the skin tone. Otherwise you will look as if you've been drinking before the interview (particularly noticeable if the TV audience is unfamiliar with the way you look). Many politicians regularly use this magic cosmetic without anyone being the wiser.

Natural Foundation　A liquid or powder foundation is applied next with a sponge so only a minimal amount is used. A colour slightly deeper than your natural skin colouring will be chosen, to make you look natural under the harsh, penetrating glare of studio lights.

Concealer　If you have dark circles under your eyes or deep lines, a concealing stick – lighter than your skin tone – is effective in eliminating shadows as well as blemishes.

Powder   A liberal dousing of translucent powder is necessary to prevent shine under the lights. Ask for a dusting of any bald patches, which can positively gleam on camera. If you have to wait a while between make-up and going on camera, and you are feeling warm, ask for your make-up to be touched up as necessary, just before filming.

Eyebrows   Your eyebrows will be combed to ensure that they do not distract attention from your eyes. You can request that a little hair gel be combed through to keep your brows in place; no viewer will ever notice. Always ask for this sort of help if you need it; some TV make-up artists don't go the extra mile for guests but are usually more helpful if you ask.

Your Hair on Television

An attractive hairstyle is vital to a successful image on camera, because your hair frames your face. As you would carefully select the right frame for a favourite picture, so, too, should you assess how well the shape, colour and texture of your own works for you, particularly on camera. Hairstyles that seem perfectly acceptable, even flattering, in real life can be a disaster on TV.

Neatness isn't enough when you appear on television. How often have you watched a man, especially a politician, who has so obviously had his hair sprayed down with hair lacquer that he looks as if he's wearing a skull-cap. You don't want your hair just to stay in place; it also needs to be flattering to your face *and* look real. Since you are unlikely to find a storm-force gale rampaging through the studio, you don't need to 'batten down the hatches' – a light spray will suffice.

If it has been some time since you had your hair restyled, consider having it done well before an important TV appearance. Your hair changes every five years or so – in texture, thickness, condition and, alas, often the hairline itself. So a style that looked quite good in your mid-twenties might be looking inappropriate, if not ridiculous, ten years on.

The more open and exposed your face, the better. Unless you have terrible ears, brush the sides back completely. Otherwise have a little hair brushing across them.

Long hair, that is, below the collar-line, looks particularly bad on TV. If you are a professional man trying to project yourself and your organisation, opt for a tidy, trim style. If you are in a less traditional industry, and your hair is long, tie it back cleanly in a ponytail.

If you now have little hair on top, don't try to maximise any remaining hair on the sides or back of your head by growing it long and brushing it across your bald pate. It rarely looks convincing. Far better to have a good haircut and powder the exposed areas to minimise shining. Also, make the most of your eyebrows. Brush them up and sideways to look fuller, using a fine comb lightly dipped in hair gel. The objective is to 'open up' your eyes and frame them as best you can with your brows.

Men with a good head of hair and a nice style, should keep it in place with hair gel, not with hair spray. Squeeze a pea-sized blob into your palm, rub your palms together so it's evenly distributed, then run your hands through your hair brushing the sides back and the top in line with your cut. Gel keeps your hair in place and allows your hair to look natural, not rigid.

Very thin hair can only be set with a fine spray; spray from underneath the hair to get a minimal lift. Avoid spraying too much on top or it will look plastered to your head – and, indeed, will be.

Glasses

Eyeglasses are often rejected by media consultants as an unnecessary inter-ference on television. Too often, we see amateurs appear in ill-fitted, unstyl-ish frames without any protective coating of the lenses to deflect the glare of studio lights. Such spectacles would damage your chances of communi-cating effectively.

But many people whom I have coached for TV are simply uncomfortable without their glasses and either cannot or do not wish to wear contact lenses. Despite how much younger and better looking Prime Minister John Major is without his glasses, they give him a sense of security. And many people – male and female – feel this way.

If this is the case for you, you must choose a pair of eyeglasses that are flattering. For tips on glasses, see Chapter Eight. However, on television you don't want them to be so fashionable that they actually wear you, not the reverse. Keep the colour neutral, with a clear bridge and no half-lenses.

The most important aspect of wearing glasses on TV is to have non-reflec-tive coated lenses to prevent the glare of the lights dazzling and hiding your eyes.

So now that you look the part, and are ready for the interview, there are a few other considerations to ensure you are seen and heard to your best advantage.

Posture

Many TV sets are furnished with low, comfortably cushioned sofas. These are a disaster for most TV novices, who tend to sit upon them as they would at home, well back and sunken. You lose all your energy and credibility when you sit naturally in such a chair or sofa on TV. The whole experience is unnatural; so, too, must be your seated posture.

Sit at the front edge of your chair, leaning very slightly forward with your back as straight as possible. If you are small and find the seat you are offered makes you lower than the presenter, insist on a higher chair with a firm seat. Yes, insist! You are the guest and you are there at their request. They need to treat you as a guest, show their gratitude that you have accepted their invitation. So make sure the conditions are as favourable as possible for you to be seen at your best.

Facial Expressions and Gestures

The atmosphere of a TV studio can be daunting even if you are not a novice. All sorts of equipment is jutting in from above and below, while various assistants fit you with a microphone, move you about and direct you. It is only natural to freeze up amid all this quick-paced activity, and to look like a deer caught in a car's headlights as soon as you appear on camera.

Take a few good deep breaths before sitting down, and smile at the presenter. Don't be distracted by cameras or attempt to talk to the camera. You are speaking with an interviewer and, possibly, other guests, so try to imagine yourself having this conversation at home or at your office. But don't allow yourself to relax; remember, you must deliver your message as you rehearsed it and try to come off as positively as possible.

If the subject is a serious one, you'll look like a goon if you smile throughout the interview. The key then, is to look serious and credible but not severe. Flash a light-hearted smile if the opportunity allows, so that viewers will warm to you.

Light-hearted interviews require almost a constant smile, even if you don't usually smile very much. My mouth, like many, turns down at the corners. So when I'm expressionless I can actually look annoyed. For me it's agony but I have learned to put on an effective smile for TV interviews, which makes me look pleasant, even if I'm feeling an idiot. Most of today's presenters are hired in part for their looks, and a key factor to their looks is their smile. They all have mouths that turn upwards!

In addition to maintaining eye contact with your interviewer, looking pleasant and sitting forward, use open gestures. When some guests are nervous they cross their arms to hug themselves which only projects a defensive image. If behind a table or desk, don't think that by keeping your hands hidden from view you are kidding anyone; you simply look unnatural without your hands on show.

It is best to keep them folded together to start with, if you are nervous, but opening them and using them will help you express your points. But don't overdo this or you'll look like a windmill and your hands will appear overly large. Also, avoid the teacher's preaching forefinger or aggressive mid-air slicing to emphasise points. Keep your palms up or slightly angled to the sides to project that you are visibly offering a position for consideration.

CHOOSING A PUBLIC LIFE

A successful career sometimes brings opportunities to become involved in community affairs from the voluntary roles like serving on a school board or hospital committee to holding an elected public office on a part-time or possibly even full-time basis.

Politicians, in particular, know that – constantly monitored by the media – they must be as concerned with image as they are with substance if they wish to have a successful, long-term career in public life, though most would publicly deny that image is important for fear that people might think they are not sufficiently serious about their jobs. Nevertheless, they do secretly focus as much attention on personal presentation as on the formulation of public policy. They know that this is the professional approach required in modern politics. The politician is the vehicle for explaining issues and proposing solutions. That vehicle packages the message and becomes the message itself.

I have been involved in politics on and off for most of my life, from street canvassing as a child in local elections to speech writing for candidates, lobbying for social causes, drafting legislation, managing national programmes and working in government. Since the televising of Parliament began in the United Kingdom in 1989, I have worked with British politicians of every political persuasion, coaching them on how to project a better image – from the clothes that they wear to preparing presentations and handling media interviews.

Anyone in public life, be it a single-issue activist or elected official, appreciates the importance of televised communication. Either they master it or they sink into obscurity. Television is a career-maker and a career-breaker. Parties and leaders must use it effectively, to win; those who don't, lose.

In America, television was first used in the public arena in the 1950s, to cover a Congressional investigation into organised crime. It turned the chairman of the proceedings, a self-deprecating, southern Senator named Estes Kefauver into a cult figure. Later, during the 1960 Presidential election between John F. Kennedy and the then Vice President Richard Nixon, the first such candidates' debate proved defeating for the arguably more experienced and better briefed Vice President. Because Nixon failed to groom himself for television, wearing the wrong colours and refusing outright to wear any make-up, he lost to the young 'upstart' Kennedy, because the latter looked more convincing to the American public on television. Kennedy had not only been dressed appropriately and had submitted to being made-up, prior to going on air, but also underwent coaching in improving his body language and gestures, to look more capable, to look like a winner.

All leading figures in modern politics have had their image advisers; not simply to write their memorable speeches and teach them acting skills to enhance their delivery, but also to advise them on dress.

- Harold Macmillan underwent a total overhaul as Prime Minister, with the advent of television coverage of British politics.

- US President Lyndon Johnson, not remembered for his good looks, had extra inches added to his shirt collars to hide his distracting adam's apple.

- Another President, Jimmy Carter, donned woolly cardigans for his fireside chats to Americans during the energy crisis in the late 1970s, to urge people to turn down their thermostats and to wear warmer clothing at home, just as he and his family were doing in the White House.

- Mikhail Gorbachev heeded advice to order suits from London's famous Savile Row, to bridge his credibility gap with western leaders. Those quality business suits were intended to inspire confidence that Gorbachev could be trusted with loans from the West, that in his own country he had equal authority to that enjoyed by his similarly clad peers in theirs. Only if this was so, could he follow through the undertakings he promised.

- Everyone worldwide watched with fascination, the gradual but profound transformation of Britain's first woman Prime Minister. Everything from how Mrs Thatcher spoke – she was coached to lower her voice and to speak more deliberately – to the colour and styling of her hair, her make-up and the style of her clothes were all fine-tuned before our eyes. Now entitled Baroness, she clearly continues to practise all that she learned in her record term of office.

- Thatcher's successor, Britain's self-confessed 'plug-ugly' John Major, has also taken advice, despite his initial protests that he would not subject himself to the image makers. The wool and polyester suits have been replaced by quality Chester Barries, the ties are no longer bought by his wife Norma at Tesco's, the blue shirts which exacerbated his beard line are now replaced by pink or soft white versions, and a non-reflective coating has been added to his glasses. The impact of these changes has been modest but it's as far as Mr Major is willing to go – at the moment.

Undeniably, his image is now more polished than when he was first cat-apulted to power.

Even Spouses are Inspected

Political Spouses, generally wives, are increasingly subjected to comment about their images and how they help or detract from the nation's image abroad. The wives get photographed together and scored according to their standing in the style stakes. Norma Major's transformation, from a quietly pretty but too conventionally dressed woman into a very stylish lady, was widely reported and approved.

First Lady Hillary Clinton underwent a substantial makeover during the 1992 Presidential campaign because her severe 'career woman' image was costing her husband votes. Functional glasses were replaced by contact lenses, her naturally mousey hair was highlighted golden blonde and her wardrobe of shapeless suits replaced by more figure-hugging knits. She even submitted her recipe for brownies against that of incumbent Barbara Bush and, surprisingly, won.

Developing a Public Image

If you are interested in preparing yourself for a role in public life, it is wise to consider what you need to change before you are in the limelight. The last thing a politician wants is for his image to become an issue, for it to appear that he needed a 'going-over' in order to be more appealing to voters. A good public image won't secure you an election, but it will help you be lis-tened to, possibly to be believed in and consequently voted for. A good image bridges gaps with voters of different backgrounds, of different ages.

The first challenge in developing an image that will work for, not against, you in public life is to remove or improve any distracting features. These might include a wild, unkempt hair style, a gap in your teeth, a pot belly, weird unconscious gestures or a poor quality voice. If you are intent on a public life, it is essential to sort out all these problems long before ever hitting a campaign trail. Once the physical problems are dealt with you need to re-appraise your clothes and grooming, as suggested throughout these pages.

Remember : all politicians of any persuasion should aim to project three things through their personal image:

- commitment
- vigour
- professionalism.

You must show commitment first and foremost to the people you intend to represent. Therefore, adapt your image, as necessary, to relate to your constituents. They need to feel comfortable with you, that you are one of them and approachable. Hence, a candidate from a rural constituency must tread through the farmers' fields appropriately dressed, in a waxed jacket and wellies. But when s/he appears on local television, s/he needs to look like a professional politician, and well able to represent local issues with the power brokers in the capital. The image must be adaptable, not in a false sense, just to send the right signals, to communicate effectively, whatever the audience.

Politicians, along with anyone in public life, must also show commitment to the policies they wish to shape. The policies are part of the organisation or party they represent. The identity of the party needs to be projected in the candidate's image just as a businessman should aim to project the corporate image.

Vigour is also vital to the success of a political candidate. He must show he has the stamina to go the distance. Margaret Thatcher did this by working inordinate hours and proving herself more able than lesser earthlings to function on very little sleep. George Bush was fanatical to show that a man in his sixties was as fit as any contender for the presidency 10 or 20 years younger.

The final goal of any candidate for public office is to show professionalism. True, off-beat anti-establishment candidates are elected from time to time, but generally, they don't remain in office for long; their eccentric style alienates too many mainstream voters. A professional image means being well-dressed, appropriate for your constituents as well as the occasion – outstanding but not out of step.

IMAGE ADVICE

Let's recap on the previous chapters. Assess your physical appearance; if you can't be objective about it, get others to tell you what two or three things need dealing with to help improve your image.

- Pay attention to your face, in particular, as this will be the main focus of attention, whether at meetings, presentations or television interviews. Is your skin in good condition or would it benefit from an occasional facial, possibly even a series of sun-lamp treatments, just to help you look more healthy.

- Visit the dental hygienist three times a year, to keep your teeth as white as possible. Consider having seriously uneven or overcrowded teeth corrected, and any broken ones capped. Your dentist will be happy to advise you.

- Make sure that your eyes are shown in the best possible light. Tweeze or wax unsightly hairs between the brows, and trim brows that are excessively thick. Have your glasses tinted with a non-reflective colourless coating to eliminate glare without competing with the colour of your eyes.

- If your hair is unruly and difficult to control, see a good stylist to advise you on a better cut, possibly a treatment such as a soft perm to make it more manageable. If you are going grey and it isn't terribly flattering, consider a rinse closer to your natural colour.

- Get fit! A lumpy, lethargic person can't fake fitness by simply picking up their pace when in the public eye. Keep trim (not slim) for your size and show a vigour that comes from eating well and getting enough rest and exercise.

- If you do feel run down, get away to a health farm for a few days. Build time into your daily diary for fresh air and some exercise, even if it is only a brisk walk at lunchtime either alone or with like-minded colleagues.

- Resist the bad habit of discussing business over a drink. All too easily, one leads to another, and while you may still feel sharp, you won't think or act sharp.

- Dress conventionally if that is what your particular profession or organisation clearly expects. But you can still avoid looking like a clone. Wear interesting ties that show you are serious but also individual.

- Look approachable. However senior your position, don't become unapproachable. Men who look too serious, take themselves too seriously, don't inspire confidences – and soon lose touch with their workforce. You can look approachable by how you sit, by your gestures and facial expressions. Don't always sit ramrod stiff in meetings or interviews. Move forward, shift slightly, tilt your head when you are supposed to be listening and smile when it is appropriate to do so. You won't lose dignity; you will gain in many ways – not least in a more convivial and co-operative working atmosphere.

- At weekends, try to give yourself a break; don't bring home a punishingly heavy workload that leaves you with no time at all in which to relax. Leave formal suits in your wardrobe and dress more casually. Now's the time to take it easy in a sports jacket with a polo-necked sweater or sports-shirt, and team them with toning trousers in fine wool. A change of pace, a change of style – that's the essence of image-building.

CHAPTER 15

GOING INTERNATIONAL

YOUR career may eventually become international, as many companies, both large and small, rely increasingly on imports and exports in order to do business. Your success in working abroad hinges largely on how well you understand how other cultures differ from your own and what effort you make to accommodate those differences.

SWOTTING UP

If planning a trip abroad, try to study ahead of time to learn as much as possible about the customs, ways of doing business and potential pitfalls. Don't rely on a pocket guide hastily purchased at the airport to give you all you need to know.

Read trade journals, international business dailies and newsheets. Contact the best university in your own country with a good department in international business and arrange to see someone who specialises in the country you plan to visit. Top commercial banks all have country desks or specialists with up-to-date information about doing business abroad. Your own embassy will have a commercial attaché locally, whom you should contact by phone or fax and, if possible, arrange to meet before your first meeting with your new business contacts.

What you need to determine is how business is done in that country. Once you've got a good feel for it, you have a much better chance of achieving your own objectives.

Here are some of the questions you will want to research ahead of time to win acceptance as quickly as possible.

1. What is the purpose of your visit?   Make sure you are clear about your own goals before you begin making appointments. If you are on a fact-finding visit, you don't need to waste the time of the top person. But if you are prepared to negotiate a deal, seeing people who have no authority is a waste of *your* time.

2. How are meetings conducted?   Find out as much as possible about the corporate culture you are visiting. How hierarchical or collegial is it? How international? Do they like everyone to participate? How much detail will be expected/appreciated?

3. How are deals done?   Much to the chagrin of many business people, some deals take time. So try to learn whether or not a deal is possible in one visit. Many westerners, particularly Americans, lose deals because they aren't prepared to invest the necessary time, including repeat visits, to make them happen.

4. How social is business?   If a lunch is planned, is it gauche or is it appropriate to discuss business? In many countries you are considered boorish if you do.

Are you likely to be invited to someone's home for dinner? If so, what would be an appropriate gift? In Europe, such subtleties as knowing whether to arrive with flowers or not, or to send them the next day, conveys how urbane you are; hence, you win extra points at the negotiating table.

If in doubt about gifts, bring something for their children, or play it safe with a book or a pen.

5. How punctual should you be?   It is fine to be up to an hour late in Spain but over five minutes in New York will cost you. Understanding acceptable punctuality in different countries conveys your respect and urbanity. Equally important is understanding the unwritten but vital codes of arrival and departure for social occasions.

6. How well will your jokes fly?   The extent to which humour is used in business is frighteningly variable. In Britain, an executive without a spark of wit is considered a dolt; in Germany, if you tell more than one joke during the business day you are a clown.

Wit and humour bear a direct relationship to the amount of honour that one needs to convey in a particular society. In countries where honour is paramount, keep your jokes under wraps. In those where self-deprecation is valued, let 'em rip.

7. What dress is acceptable?   Just to consider the climate is never enough in planning your travel wardrobe for a business trip abroad. If in doubt, think *conservatively*. Dress as if you were to meet the most important person in your company, and that s/he is about 60 years old. You don't want to look flashy, just impressive – and always professional. Take no risks.

Now that we've considered all the areas you need to research ahead, let's home in closer on just a few of these points, so you are fully aware of the sort of pitfalls that await you if you don't do this thoroughly.

LEARNING RIGHT FROM WRONG

The vexing problem about trying to figure out how to handle yourself abroad is that no *one* approach is right. The challenge is to learn how things are done *there*. You have your own understanding about how meetings work, how to handle yourself over dinner, how to negotiate and so on, based on what works in your own culture. But what works elsewhere may require the reverse tactics to succeed.

When meeting people for the first time, we struggle initially to find common ground. We do this through language, dress, manners, humour, mutual acquaintances, opinions – and we aim to relate to each other as quickly as we can. Hence, if we don't speak the language at all, dress inappropriately, use offensive behaviour, manners or humour, voice contrary opinions, are of a different age and sex, communication becomes a herculean task, if not an impossible one.

It's a Small World After All

We all have telephones and faxes and can leap from one continent to another with little notice, in little time. Some foreign places seem quite like home, where you can watch your favourite TV programme, buy your regular soft drink, or find the same clothes as you have at home. It is easy to get lulled into thinking that such familiar things mean that the cultures are similar. In Tokyo, for example, you can watch CNN, buy a Coca Cola and find Levis as well as Calvin Klein jeans but the differences between the Japanese lifestyle and way of doing business with those of America couldn't be further apart.

As 'small' as the world is becoming through modern communication and international marketing we are witnessing a resurgence of cultural assertiveness. Futurist John Naisbitt said in the 1982 edition of the international publication *Megatrends* that in the future 'the Swedes will become more Swedish, the Chinese more Chinese. And the French, God help us, more French.'

The recession of the late 1980s and early 90s forged a bunker mentality in many countries. If Americans didn't buy a car that was made in the USA they were personally contributing to the national debt. The German Bundesbank would hike its interest rates, to the chagrin of every other European country, to protect German economic interests at the expense and outcry of its neighbours. To 'Buy British' became the clarion call of the UK's largest retailer Marks & Spencer, as if buying anything else was unpatriotic.

We are all proud of our own nationality and culture as well as our business acumen. But you can earn enormous credit when you show respect for the culture and successes of others who are equally proud. When travelling or working abroad don't flaunt your differences, keep them to yourself or risk being mistaken for an arrogant chauvinist.

BARRIERS TO COMMUNICATION

Ask most seasoned international travellers what is the key barrier to communication and language will top the list. Even if those you plan to visit speak yours as a second language, make an effort to speak the minimum of courtesies and salutations in theirs, to convey your desire to communicate. Even if you stumble and make a hash of the pronunciation you will be appreciated for making the effort.

Remember that even if your associates can speak your language, they don't necessarily think in it the way you do. All sorts of subtleties are missed when we don't speak in our native tongue. So, don't assume everything is understood.

Perhaps the greatest barriers to communication when mixing with foreigners are the non-verbal messages we send through our body language, dress and manners. Here, there can be profound differences in cultures and if you travel without first finding out what they are, you could ruin your chances of doing business with a client, for good.

Body Language

How we communicate non-verbally is learned, imitated or simply instinctive. We each have our own body personality but temper it according to the cultural mores of where we live and work.

Territory

Depending on where you grew up, how close your family was, whether you are a man or a woman affects the amount of 'personal territory' you need when dealing with other people. Many of us need to be close, even to touch frequently, to feel we are communicating, while others need to maintain a distance in order to feel comfortable.

Comfort is your prime consideration when communicating at home or dealing on your own turf. When travelling abroad, you need to subjugate your own preferences in favour of others. If you prefer keeping at a distance yet in the host country all nationals huddle closely (especially Arabs and Latins), you'll be misunderstood, even mistrusted, if you stay apart. Observe their behaviour, try to mirror it with your own, and you will relate to them better. A little personal discomfort is a small price to pay in breaking down important barriers to help you communicate effectively.

Handshakes and Greetings

In every culture, the first three minutes are vital. This is when we size each other up, and evaluate each other's background and success. When abroad, if you fail with your introduction you most likely won't get another chance.

Individuals from different cultures shake hands differently. Don't shrug your shoulders and say, 'Why bother. They'll have to take me as I come'. Why ruin your chances before you even open your mouth?

In Europe alone there are many varieties of handshakes. The French give you one firm, deliberate stroke. In Scandinavia, you get two firm strokes then are firmly pushed away, alerting you to keep your distance. In Italy and Greece, they shake for up to a minute, giving you maybe half-a-dozen relaxed strokes. If you try to rush them, you will be considered uncouth.

In the Far East, you'll need to perfect your bowing – for Japan, Thailand and Malaysia, among other countries. They have adopted the initial handshake for business purposes but otherwise hate physical contact.

Men can show respect and hospitality to female guests by offering a deliberate, not just polite, handshake. The only time you are advised to hold back is when you meet the spouse of a business associate abroad, where it might be considered impolite to shake hands. Check with a knowledgeable local expert before any major social function.

When introducing others, present people to the most senior/important person. After being presented yourself, work your way around the gathering, making an effort to meet everyone, conveying that everyone there is important to you.

In many countries, the introduction is followed by the presentation of business cards. If you come from a country where business cards are treated with indifference, don't assume this will be so when working abroad. Before an important trip, have yours translated so that the flip side is in the local language. Present that side to your host. Be sure to admire the cards proffered to you. Much time and effort is given to the design and printing of business cards, so convey some appreciation.

Check to see if the country you are visiting is impressed by titles and degrees (e.g. France, Germany, Switzerland, Japan, Korea, Singapore, China, the Arab Nations, and many South American countries). If so, add any that you can legitimately claim as your own.

Gestures

Most western cultures encourage the use of gestures as part of communication, but interpreting them can be tricky even when dealing with people in your own culture. The person may simply be responding to some physical change, such as feeling an itch, the cold, slight indigestion, that causes them to gesture or move instinctively. But it is far more difficult to interpret gestures correctly when working in a foreign culture, distinctly different from your own. You are therefore advised to read up, speak to experts, and become as familiar as possible with how your own natural gestures might be misinterpreted. Many a western businessman has been dismissed as a peasant when travelling to the Arab world, simply because he sat showing the soles of his shoes.

As well as learning what to watch out for in your own behaviour, you also need to learn what you might misinterpret. In Japan, for instance, business people often think they have clinched a deal because they were repeatedly told 'Yes', with lots of positive smiling faces and nodding heads. However, that may not be the case. The Japanese avoid confrontation at all costs. Asking for an answer straight out requires them to agree, so that you feel 'harmonious'. They see no problem in getting back to you later with a reverse decision they had to take for spiritual as well as commercial benefit of the company.

If in doubt about your gestures, however enthusiastic you might be about your project, present it calmly and try to convey your thoughts through your words. Repeat yourself or rephrase things to reinforce key points. Convey your belief and determination verbally, rather than risk insulting someone by unintentionally using unfortunate gestures.

In summary, you *can* succeed in doing business abroad if you prepare ahead. The effort is well worth while. You will enjoy yourself more if you know that you are communicating effectively, and success in dealing with other nationalities can only bring you further success in your career – at home and abroad.

CONCLUSION: 'TO THINE OWN SELF BE TRUE'

We have now run the gamut of what it takes to present the best of yourself in your career, covering the tangible as well as the intangible. From the colour, style, fit and quality of clothes that will make you look professional and attractive, to grooming your voice, presentation skills, keeping your body fit and putting the right foot forward when dealing on foreign soil.

I trust that you accept that what has worked well for you thus far in your career might not be sufficient to help you in the future. Fine-tuning is needed throughout your career; so don't rest on your laurels. Do something about those weaknesses in your own image, those roadblocks to further success.

Above all, remember that the packaging and the art of self-presentation must be true to the real you inside. An improved image can give you a tremendous boost in confidence. But it's up to you – your skills, expertise and personality – to see the job through. If my advice helps to get you through doors previously closed to you, over hurdles you would have never contemplated jumping, then I will consider my efforts have been worthwhile. I wish you well.

TO THINE OWN SELF BE TRUE

BIBLIOGRAPHY

PRESENTATION SKILLS

How to Talk So People Listen, Sonya Hamlin (Thorsons)
Janner's Complete Speechmaker, Greville Janner QC, MP (Century Business)
Never Be Nervous Again, Dorothy Sarnoff (Crown Books, NY)
Personal Power, Philippa Davies (Piatkus)
Power Communication Skills, Dr Susan Baile (Career Track Publications, NY)
Power Presentations, Brody and Kent (Wiley)
Powerspeak, Dorothy Leeds (Piatkus)
Silent Messages, Professor A Mehrabian (University College, Los Angeles)

HANDLING TV

Communications and the Modern World (Macmillan, NY)
Understanding Media, Marshall McLuhan (Ark Paperbacks)
You Are The Message, Roger Ailes and John Krausmar (Dow Jones-Irwin)
Your Public Best, Lillian Brown (New Market Press)

CAREER DEVELOPMENT

A Passion for Excellence, Tom Peters (Warner Books, NY)
A Passion for Leadership, Tom Peters (Warner Books, NY)
Breaking the Glass Ceiling, Ann Morrison, etc., Centre for Creative Leadership
   (Addison-Wesley)
The 7 Habits of Highly Effective People, Stephen R. Covey (Simon & Schuster)

MEN'S IMAGE

A Gentleman's Wardrobe, Paul Keers (Weidenfeld)
Clothes and The Man, Alan Flusser (Villard Books)

Dress for Excellence, Lois Fenton (Rawson Associates, NY)
How a Man Ages, Curtis Pesmen (Ballantine/Esquire Press)
The Style of an Englishman, Nicky Smith (Michael Joseph)
The Winner's Style, Ken Karpinski (Acropolis)

CORPORATE IMAGE

Corporate Identity, Wally Olins (Thames & Hudson)
The Business of Image, Nicholas Jenkins (Kogan Page)

PUBLIC IMAGE

Images of Power, Brendan Bruce (Kogan Page)

CROSS CULTURAL UNDERSTANDING

Eurobarometer: Public Opinion in the European Community
    (published by the EC)
Culturgram for the 90s, Brigham Young University, Center for International
    Studies, Provo, Utah
Going International, Lennie Copeland and Lewis Griggs (Penguin, NY)
Guide des Bonnes Mannières et du Protocole en Europe, Jacques Gandouin
    (Pergamon Books, Fixot)
Mind Your Manners, John Mole (The Industrial Society, London)
The Art of Japanese Management, Pascale and Athos (Simon and Schuster, NY)
The Travellers Guide to Middle Eastern and North African Customs and Manners,
    E. Devine and N. Braganti (St. Martin's Press, NY)
The World Class Executive, Neil Shesanow (Rawson Associates, NY)

Picture Credits

All shirts by Charles Tyrwhitt

Page 38, suits by Yves St Laurent, ties by Christian Dior (top right) and Turnbull & Asser (bottom right)

Page 40, photo of Sylvester Stallone © Rex Features, photo of Linford Christie © Allsport

All clothes on pages 41, 43, 45, 47, 49 and 51 from Selfridges

Page 42, photo of Paul Hogan © Rex Features

Page 44, photo of Kenneth Branagh © Rex Features

Page 46, photo of Bill Clinton © Rex Features

Page 48, photo of Timothy Dalton © Rex Features

Page 50, photo of Nigel Mansell © Allsport

Page 56, *left:* suit by Yves St Laurent at Selfridges, tie by Turnbull & Asser; *right:* suit and tie by Next

Page 57, *left and centre:* model's own suit and tie; *right:* suit by Jaeger at Selfridges, tie by Liberty, pocket handkerchief by Turnbull & Asser

Page 65, *left:* suit by Chester Barrie at Selfridges; *right:* suit on hanger by Gieves & Hawkes

Page 68, photos courtesy of Next

Page 78, navy suit by Chester Barrie at Selfridges, tie by Gucci, handkerchief by Turnbull & Asser; grey suit and coloured suit by Hugo Boss at Austin Reed, ties by Turnbull & Asser

Page 80, pin-stripe suit by Austin Reed, tie by Turnbull & Asser; Prince of Wales check suit by Gieves & Hawkes at Selfridges, tie and pocket handkerchief by Turnbull & Asser

Page 82, sports jacket and trousers by Yves St Laurent at Selfridges; dinner suit by Austin Reed, waistcoat by Tom Gilbey

Page 83, photos courtesy of Charles Tyrwhitt

Page 95, accessories from Selfridges

Page 97, photo courtesy of The Pen Shop

Page 98, photo courtesy of Austin Reed

Page 103, *bottom left:* tie by Turnbull & Asser; *bottom right:* tie by Gucci.
   (Both shirts by Charles Tyrwhitt, as elsewhere)

Page 104, jacket by Louis Feraud at Selfridges, shirt by Gap

Page 109, jacket by Yves St Laurent at Selfridges, cotton polo by Gap

Page 114, photo courtesy of Reebok

Page 124, photo © Telegraph Colour Library

Pages 134–5, he wears suit by Hugo Boss at Austin Reed, she wears jacket and
   skirt by JH Collectibles at Selfridges and scarf from Options at Austin Reed

Page 138, photo © Tony Stone Worldwide

Page 140, photo © Telegraph Colour Library

Page 149, photo © BBC News and Current Affairs

INDEX

MORE FROM CMB IMAGE CONSULTANTS

YOUR PERSONAL COLOUR SWATCHES

You can order our handy shopping guide to your best colours by requesting information about our Personal Colour Swatches. You will receive a set of over 30 fabric swatches representing the best colours for your suits, shirts and ties. This colour wallet can help you sort out your existing wardrobe as well as avoid future shopping mistakes.

PERSONAL IMAGE CONSULTATIONS

CMB's top image consultants can offer more advice on your image so you feel confident that you are presenting yourself at your best.

An individual consultation will show you colours and styles for work as well as casual wear and how to combine colours and patterns to achieve a look that works for you.

Our aim is to make selecting clothes easy. You receive your own style guide full of notes as well as a wallet of 60 colour fabric swatches to use when shopping. To put the theory into practice, or for men with time restrictions, CMB can organise individual shopping trips.

CMB PRODUCTS

CMB also has a skincare range using essential aromatherapy oils for men and women. If you are interested, tick the box on the Information Request form for a copy of our catalogue.

CMB SEMINARS ON PROJECTING SUCCESS

For organisations keen to present their best image, CMB conduct corporate training seminars in personal image, etiquette and presentation.

For further details on our services or products, please complete and return the freepost information request form below. Alternatively, ring us directly on 071 627 5211

CMB Image Consultants, 66 Abbey Business Centre, Ingate Place, London SW8 3NS

INFORMATION REQUEST FORM

Please send me information on the following:

(tick the boxes as necessary)

My Personal Colour Swatches ☐

Personal Image Consultation for Men ☐

CMB's Product Catalogue ☐

CMB's Corporate Seminars ☐

NAME: _____ *(please print)*

ADDRESS _____

_____

DAYTIME TELEPHONE NO: _____

CMB Image Consultants
FREEPOST
London SW8 3BR